ALL MINDS
ARE EQUAL

Melike

To hard-working and innocent parents.

CONTENTS

In the drowsy dark caves of the mind
dreams build their nest with fragments
dropped from day's caravan.

--Rabindranath Tagore

CHAPTER 1: BELLA

My mother enjoyed interpreting dreams, she must have felt blessed to have my big sister talking about her endless dreams at breakfast time. Along this similar vein, the two of them would continue until they finished their last drop of tea, while an unimpressed me always claimed that I had unregistered dreams to get out of the senseless situation, as I called it. I often watched my sister's boisterous steps on her way to school after a rosy prediction for her day based on the dreams, and wondered if a dizzy adventure of an unconscious night can help us to be a more optimistic person during the day.

Logically I didn't expect my waking life was controlled by night journeys, but did dread those unnerving dark hours when I had to battle demons as my sweet dreams turned into nightmares. To make sure that I wasn't surrounded by the singing skeletons and floating ghosts once nightfall hits, I had to keep a little light on all night in my bedroom at a time when the monthly electricity bill could cost an arm or leg in China.

Driven by a passion for unsolved mysteries, Mother tried to interpret my dreams too, and claimed she saw me often smiling in my sleep, something I always observed my daughters do later in life. It was at my university days, after dinner my entire family would gather next to the TV since staring at the little box was the only entertainment at that era. I joined them on the long sofa and would doze off unapologetically well before the news was over. In view of resting with my eyes and ears comfortably shut, I ought to smile contentedly.

No amount of music from the TV, occasional cheer, gasp or nonstop dialogue, including the translation from Chinese into Uyghur, could halt my power nap. Luckily all programs were terminated before 10pm, and when everyone was getting ready for bed, I would be up to do my homework. I was amazed that the daunting mathematical problems suddenly became easy to solve in those quiet night hours. With worry off the table, I would sleep tight then rise early to attend the first lecture at the next morning.

One day I finally decided to stop Mother from pestering me with her fortune telling nonsense. She wasn't amused that I didn't want to absorb the wisdom received from dreams, until I told

Mother about a woman who got up in the morning to inform her husband that they would argue on that day. 'Why should we argue?' asked her confused husband. The woman apparently saw cherries in her dream and that was the symbol of an imminent argument. It wasn't too hard to fulfil her dream - the argument unfolded as she insisted. Her husband found it absurd to have a row on purpose, regardless she was intoxicated with the accuracy of her dream. Mother admitted it could be true reluctantly, but I wanted her to look back at the joke and laugh at ease later.

This brings me to my second point, do we use theory to justify our actions or modify our behaviour to fit the theory? I never believed that the greatest scientist of our time, Albert Einstein, could ever ask us to change the facts if they don't fit the theory. But the very irresponsible psychotherapist I met in the Donald Winnicott Centre, who was more of an amateur artist than a serious scientist, did try her best to adjust my life experience to fit her theory.

Aside from her rather churlish suspicion, the psychotherapist went as far as to reimagine the historical details from my early past to carry her practice to excess. According to her I chose to only remember the pleasant events of my budding life. For it would be a dead end of the psychoanalytic theory to accept a happy childhood led me to bring up children with developmental disorders. I watched in disbelief at just how she tried to set up a dubious detour that specifically applied in finding the wrongs with my upbringing.

I am one of those people who don't thrive on the sympathy of strangers, psychotherapists included. It was the health visitor who arranged me to see the *expert of child development*, as she called them and strangely there was a dream to start up the entire saga. I was seven months pregnant and it was surreal to watch that one night my daughter more or less walked out from my womb. She didn't just look like a five-year-old, she was also demanding to go to the cinema with me immediately, as if she had been steadfastly studying the world before her unscheduled entrance.

I was intrigued but had to quietly follow her as she was gregariously greeting everyone in the street. In the cinema she watched the film and I watched her only. Much as I was searching for the traces of my DNA on her features, I was petrified to see her eyes were uncharacteristically small. Could my child have been swapped when I delivered her at home with no one around? 'No, it can't be!', I screamed. I woke up worried, my husband tried to assure me that it was only a nightmare. I wanted to discuss my dream with him, but he dismissively rolled over to the other side and promised me to talk about it in the morning.

At breakfast time, my husband talked casually

about the fact that it was not unusual for a first-time expectant mother to experience such anxiety, then unhesitatingly left home to see his patients in his GP surgery, supposedly to deal with more meaningful complaints. How I wished my mother was here to interpret my dream and help me to rein my racing thoughts until the arrival of the big moment soon. Now left on my own, I tried to make sense of the events in my dream from my own perspective. I know why I saw a girl, since I longed for a daughter with a yearning desire for as long as I could remember.

I was forbidden from playing with dolls by my strictly religious father during my childhood. Not a single doll I ever possessed – not even was I allowed to keep the doll I received as a present from our guests. 'Muslim girls don't play with dolls!' Father proclaimed, simultaneously handing the present back to the stunned guests. From those young years, I already realised religion is full of contradictions. Father was fond of photos and watched TV, but merely singled out dolls as human image. That was why I set my heart on having a daughter one day so I could braid her long brown hair and dress her up with the prettiest garments in the world.

Making sense of the rest of the dream was not such a straightforward process anymore, but I could still relate to having a five-year-old child instead of an infant girl. It sounded like my favourite childhood character Nezha from the famous Chinese novel *The Creation of the Gods* (Fengshen Yanyi). Nezha was born a walking, talking child after his mother carried him for three years and six months in her womb. I loved Nezha's Wind Fire Wheels, it was like he was constantly flying to help people to get justice.

Of course he was part of the bigger plot in overthrowing the corrupt emperor, but his conflicts with his father makes for an unpleasant reading, especially the bit where he had to commit suicide by returning his flesh and bone to his parents. Here is Chinese culture in its most revealing and vivid display, including considering parents as the ones who own your life.

Luckily it is a historic fantasy novel, and Nezha was brought back to life, he was even able to reconcile with his father later. There were two dreams which played prominent roles in Nezha's life: the first one was at the night before his birth, his mother dreamed a Taoist priest told her to have the child by pushing an object inside her belly. The second message was communicated through Nezha after his death, as he asked his bereaving mother to build a temple to rest his soul in the Chinese tradition. Mother's love triumphs over father's hate! It was the temple which allowed the recreation of his body and finally reclaim his place in the real world.

Indulging in my childhood memories has always

been a pleasure, but to understand why my daughter in my dream looked so different from me was not easy. Years later when I recounted the dream to the psychotherapist, she thought that reflected my suffering during my early years in China. She would, wouldn't she? After all, the theory of psychotherapy is narrowly built on digging out every single historic grudge of ours, no matter how deep it is buried in our very unreliable memory compartments.

There are people who unfortunately are encouraged to indulge in those memory-inspired sorrows, never able to move on or do something productive in their remaining lives. I happen to believe a lot of excruciating traumas from the past were marinated from the very trivial ones with prompting from many psychotherapists. Rather than letting the unalterable remembrance hurt us from within, it is better to accept that life isn't all plain sailing and plant a *green tree in heart* to *bring in singing birds*.

Besides the psychotherapist couldn't be more wrong, my life in Harbin was a pure bliss, even the Cultural Revolution could not dampen my joyous spirits for long. There were many rosy moments in my life I could look back on, but the one I indulged the most during my childhood was spending a few hours each day with the street book vendors following my brother. It is like an outdoor library, after paying a few pennies we were allowed to browse through all the books for as long as we wanted.

I loved those children's picture books, called *Xiaoren Shu* in China, a direct translation would be *Little people's books*. I think it is phrased as little people instead of children's book simply because the books are tiny, and the palm-sized books were skilfully illustrated with miniature historic figures. It is black and white with subtitles, which are designed to retell many stories from famous Chinese classic novels to young people.

These tiny books allowed me not to stretch my imagination too far, as all those interesting heroes, mythological figures and historic legends were painstakingly depicted in a child-friendly manner. Although the Cultural Revolution put an end to this hugely entertaining trade which certainly boasts a long history, by then I was already old enough to delve into the real things, the books those Xiaoren Shu inspired me, even made me hungry to read.

I was too young to be scarred by the Cultural Revolution, which was only violent for the first couple of years. I don't know how many eleven-year-olds took up the free tour on crowded trains. My big sister and my brother hopped on the bandwagon (literally and figuratively), while one was elated in Beijing to see Chairman Mao in flesh very up close, at the same time the other one was traumatized by being robbed of all his possessions in Dalian.

I was rather pleased not to have to join the fanatic crowd and worry about food, drink and some other more basic human needs on a tightly packed train, instead I cosily carried on my reading at home to enter the magical past in my favourite books. The past sounded so much more exciting than that time I was growing up, yet reassuringly more peaceful like distant stars.

My modest and neighbour-friendly parents also helped us to get through the revolution peacefully, as we had a lucky escape to not be targeted by the Red Guards as an anti-revolutionary family, which was particularly likely as the only Uyghur family in the entire city of Harbin. By the time the Cultural Revolution was mercifully over and university exams were resumed, I was able to start studying civil engineering at the age of 22, a reasonable age to start a new chapter in my life by my own standard.

Elated by my dream finally coming true, I forgot I wasn't a teenager anymore and had the best time of my life in the university. That probably can explain why I went to study in Open University at the age of 53 to experience that euphoria again. I remember the shocked impression on my classmate's face when she learned my age. For my part, I was satisfied. After all, I learnt a lot about infants' behaviour and graduated with an advanced diploma in child development as well as an MA in education.

Dream aside, my need for my mother's presence became all the more pressing during the moment when my daughter was born two months later, as my husband merely became an extra invalid in the hospital room. Instead of holding my hands to help me to conquer my fear, he went through the entire delivery process insufferably pacing with two hands in his pocket, just short of whistling, but inarticulately mumbling something like "You can do it."

I hopelessly watched him gang up with the midwife and the other two doctors to insist the exhausted me didn't qualify for further assistance. Eventually the slowing down of my daughter's heartbeat gave the medics no choice but to respond to my plea. My daughter was born with the help of forceps. I felt vindicated for being this wimp who forced the doctors to speed up my delivery, since a few weeks later I was horrified to learn from a TV program that prolonged delivery can cause birth asphyxia, with serious damage to the baby's brain.

Finally I had myself a daughter, and she looked perfect. Holding Bella in my arms was certainly the happiest moment of my life, especially as the dove-eyed her looked nothing less than an epitome of a typical Uyghur beauty. We all heard the claim that the newborns on magazine covers are at least three months old, with no birthmark or wrinkles, but that was Bella from the moment she came out from my womb. Even my husband gasped about how beautiful Bella was. Soon I discovered that the pregnancy and delivery are the easy bits in the process of starting a family - to bring the children up is a whole new challenge of its own.

First I was worried that Bella was avoiding eye contact from birth, until I learnt that babies can't see clearly until they are six weeks old, let alone worry about being stared at by me at all times. Soon my husband came up with some other new worrying claim that he thought Bella was squint, hence suggested that we see an eye specialist as early as possible. The specialist assured us that all abnormalities could become normal very soon, as Bella grows.

According to her Bella was still learning how to coordinate her two eyes, i.e. to look at objects with both eyes at the same time instead of resourcefully stealing a look of something else from a corner of one eye only. It was a relief for me but my husband didn't look convinced.

I gradually learnt to cope with my husband's unfounded anxiety and had to set my own aside: a 50-year-old GP and first-time father, his heart was ruling over his knowledgeable brain. He later told me that his fear for Bella's eyes spawned from his sister's squint eyes. As someone who once failed to notice a colleague was limping for three years, I also failed to perceive that my sister-in-law can't focus her two eyes on the same object.

After all, my music teacher sister-in-law's career is never impeded by her eyesight, I would not worry if Bella did inherit her weakness to a certain degree. Gradually we learnt how to separate side issues from genuine problems, and it was Bella's speech that started dominating our concern. As it became obvious by the time Bella was eighteen months old that she was not really talking like other toddlers.

Now looking back I can clearly see that there was no babbling, no pointing and she could squat for up to an hour in the garden staring at one little spot, presumably at wiggly worms. As her parents we had endless discussions until one day I read about a story of an autism sufferer from *The Times*. Now maybe anyone can tell you something about autism, but 30 years ago it was a rare medical condition that was not widely discussed as it is today.

Not satisfied with the definition from the Oxford dictionary, I turned to look for its Chinese meaning and felt enlightened to realise that it is called *Locked-in-self disorder*. As always, the Chinese prefer to use an explanatory name for definitions, like calling saffron *Tibetan red flower*. It is not to be confused with locked-in syndrome which is a neurological disorder. Whereas the Chinese translation of this illness have the unmistakable word *combination* in addition to the term *syndrome* for definition.

The definition that autistic people prefer to be locked into their own world voluntarily gave me hope that I could get Bella out of her isolated world. My husband started reading about autism from the few books available at that time, especially the one which was more or less considered as the Bible for this disorder.

Uta Frith's book was filled with anecdotes, some of which could be traced back to 12th century monastery in England. One thing my husband learned from his reading was that autistic sufferers are all the same, no matter where they are born or how they were brought up. Later, after meeting many autistic children, I can safely say that they are all different, since the social background and their upbringings can significantly alter their behaviour.

By the time the health visitor discovered something was not right, Bella was almost three years old. She suggested a hearing test despite my assurance that what Bella has is perfect in that department, as she was never startled to see me to appear in front of her like deaf children usually do.

According to my mother-in-law, who looked after Bella until she was seven months old, Bella reacted differently towards footsteps from my husband or mine. I should believe her observations. A mother of five and grandmother of another five children, my mother-in-law must had reached a sufficient level of expertise in this subject to warrant her observations. Later, in reception class, Bella's teacher also was impressed by her ability of discovering patterns, which many of her classmates failed to uncover.

For me Bella has undoubtedly been equipped with a better hearing than mine to start her life with. She always suddenly ran back to her room while we were having our breakfast in the kitchen. After following her I would discover *Thomas the Tank Engine* was on her little TV screen, she could hear the theme tune while I was busy eating.

She also never missed *EastEnders's* theme tune which I was watching then. To my disappointment, no one else took my reservation seriously, my husband talked about the possibility of some hidden hearing problem. Bella's nursery warned me to get prepared for the discovery of more complicated hearing ailments to my disbelief.

I wasn't surprised that the hearing test didn't detect any abnormality in Bella's auditory nerves, but it became an excuse for the health visitor to pursue further assessment. My husband agreed for the additional investigation instantly without consulting me or at least making some necessary enquiries of his own. He failed to understand why I was so furious. He thought the only way to sort out Bella's problem was to have her labelled.

I think deep inside, my husband was honestly worried that Bella would grow up with a speech impairment.

With many disconnected words Bella could use at her disposal, she rarely used them for communicational purposes. Besides Bella didn't like asking why or what - she might look puzzled initially on an object but always pursued her own research. So while the big, wide world around me was trying to find a way to turn Bella into a standard textbook child, I was in awe of her capabilities as a fairer, calmer and brainier version of myself and somebody I always aspired to be.

The many anecdotes I read kept me informed and not to be easily swayed or wilfully misled. With newly acquired knowledge, I frequently ignored the many useless and even potentially harmful pieces of advice. This included the speech therapist's order not to count further with Bella, after I boasted that she could count up to 40 already. Finding myself facing motherhood in my late thirties allowed me to trust my instinct more, since I did become aware of the fact that the plethora of information around us could be biased and far from the truth.

Gradually I started noticing a pattern which was that as parents we always focus on what our children can do and try to help them to develop and reach their potential in that direction, whilst the health professionals and even teachers always tend to exaggerate what children can't do and try to fix those so called problems by killing off children's creativity.

During one of my very few visits to the speech therapist with Bella, I noticed a chatty little girl about three-years-old walked out from the consultation room with her mother. Out of curiosity I asked the speech therapist about the need of an articulate child to come to see her. 'Oh, she says yes to everything ' was the answer. 'Such as?' I pressed on. 'If you ask her are you a girl she says yes, then if the question is about her being a boy, her reply will be yes again.'

She would learn from her peers very soon that she can't be a boy and a girl at the same time when she would only be allowed to use girls' toilets in school. But the speech therapist didn't agree with me, by carrying on with Bella's session she made it clear that she was the only person in that room to help the children out of their gender dilemma or maybe other serious issues too.

If only I knew that little girl and her mother, I would have suggested for them to get out of this *ministry of disinformation* and watch the highly entertaining *Sesame Street* episodes to pick up the art of answering. There was a story about an inept king who ended up having no ice-cream, being tickled and even had snow dumped on his head, all because he kept answering *no* to questions started with if he minded any of these miseries to happen to him.

A visit from a superhero named *Yes Man* didn't change his fate, as the clever servants started asking if they could have the king's ice-cream instead. As a result, the tickling and dumping snow on the king's head continued as usual too, as the king kept mindlessly saying *yes* to encourage the cruelties. It was only after another visit by the superhero *No Man* that the king understood the necessity to say both *yes* and *no* according to the circumstances. Finally the king was able to live happily ever after just by giving the right answer for the ever-changing questions. The tickling and dumping snow on his head stopped, and the king was able to have his ice-cream too.

With a mother's doubting and questioning eyes, I subsequently figured we were also wasting our time with the speech therapist. We were undoubtedly losing our race against time to help Bella to develop her speech, since one might become idle and indolent by expecting miracles from the speech therapist alone. Besides, if you try to see through the purpose for us traveling there, the therapy is based on the ridiculous assumption that I couldn't even spare an hour per week to play with Bella. Watching the way they conduct their therapy, I couldn't fail to notice the fact that Bella was being constantly assessed.

It started irritating me in a time when I was plagued with worries and desperate to find a way to help Bella. Then when I ditched the therapy one week, the speech therapist begged us to go back so that her student could complete her course work. This confirmed my strong suspicion that we were helping them all along. How could repeatedly pretending to wash a naked doll stimulate Bella to talk? With another baby daughter who needed my constant attention at home and seeing Bella was missing her nursery which was packed with activities for six hours a day, I finally reached the conclusion that speech therapy was not for Bella.

After I sufficiently experienced speech therapy and shunned it, I was ready to ignore the extra assessment in the Donald Winnicott Centre for Bella too. Harder to address was my husband's enthusiasm as he was expecting an outright answer from there. Even all my scepticism failed to prepare me to witness the assessment being nothing more than a folly of the blame game, and *only manners deter me from a tu quoque.*

It all started after the psychotherapist tried her best to make me accept that I had a miserable childhood to finally become this refrigerator mother and took away the speech from my child. It became gradually obvious that to divulge my entire personal life to her was a waste of time: I wasn't meant to be blissfully happy during my tender years with very caring parents. Whenever sensing my recollection was about to lead to a happy ending, the psychotherapist would divert me to a different topic so that my gratified childhood wouldn't emerge into light. The actual events apparently frustrated her, she tried to blur my joyous memories with her preferred melancholy severity.

After a great deal of failed effort to replace my early rainbow with her preferred dark cloud, the psychotherapist looked pensive, while the little girl within me was screaming to get away from her mean presence and go to hug my loving parents in the distant land.

There was another girl with her confused mother who were warmly received by all health professionals in the team. Apart from the psychologist and psychotherapist, there was also an occupational therapist, a nurse and a paediatrician. They must have felt particularly empowered when the mother begged them to tell her if at any stage of her life, the daughter would be able to live a normal life on her own. As I expected, the well-pleased team was nonetheless unable to offer a definite answer to the star-struck mother. Even the psychotherapist, with her propensity to exaggeration, didn't play God on this occasion. Yet she couldn't hide her dismay for not having me ask them about the keynote of Bella's life.

Not that life for me is just a *Que Sera Sera*, a whatever it will be situation, I happen to believe that the greatest resources of mankind are within us. At the end of the day, it was up to Bella and me to overcome this first hurdle in her life with the uplifting strength within our reach. I know Bella was determined to try hard, and I could vacillate between learning about child development and guiding Bella out of her obscure world. We could definitely be masters of Bella's destiny by searching and discovering the ways to overcome all uncertainties.

One week seemed not long enough for the assessment team to deal with a defiant mother who freakishly voiced an opinion. We were asked to come back next week to hear their all-important conclusion. The fact that my GP husband had to work at those hours was not the least of their concern. 'Both of you have to be present and without your baby daughter' was their imposing sharp order.

Our younger daughter Esin was a ten-month-old adorable baby then. She always attracted a lot of attention with her gorgeous smile, but was obviously considered as a nuisance by the psychotherapist during our discourse. Seeing Esin enjoying herself quietly on my lap during our dialogue must be beyond the bounds of her reason!

I turned down their appointment, but unexpectedly a letter with an alternative date arrived. So they could be polite when necessary, as they went as far as ready to find a babysitter for Esin in their premises. The determination they had shown to gain my attention was impressive, but wouldn't help Bella to talk. It was strange to see that they were eager to offer therapy to me, which I certainly could do without. Peculiarly my husband was still willing to accept their complete disregard of our rights as a pure and real support.

Such is the prominence of the psychotherapist's viewpoint to my deluded husband, and in that regard he never ceased believing that an elixir from her was capable of initiating speech for Bella. Except he refused to attend the meeting on his own, since the fact that I was the star of the show was perfectly notable to him too. His past could remain as an illusion, but mine had to be thoroughly discussed, arbitrarily modified and wholeheartedly denounced by them. As if life can only be revealed by excessively musing over our past!

Instead of being part of their counterproductive plot, I moved on towards my future priorities by accomplishing my vision for Bella with great labour. After dedicating every spare hour from my life to play and talk to her, I was exhilarated with the fortuitous gains which progressed Bella in the right direction.

I was brought up in the despotism of the culturally revolutionary China - listen to the party and Chairman Mao was our mantra. The recollections of my pre-Cultural Revolution school days were still joyous, it was between the age of eleven to twenty-one years old life became unbearably boring and more restricted, especially for the first couple of years. Girls all had short hair, wearing khaki-coloured jackets and were never seen without a little red book in our hand. Then the fatigue set in, no one would hold a pair of scissors in the street corner to cut off your bourgeoisie long hair anymore.

Suddenly we could grow out our hair, some girls even ended up with cascades of glossy tresses falling over their waist. Some others managed to get jobs in the cities despite initially being sent away to be country farmers. Seeing my big sister finally entered university after completing her compulsory two years re-education in a factory, I learnt all bad things do come to an end and it is important to keep your soul smiling.

However, the many lies we were told during those chaotic years did make me rather wary and chary. I tend to question other people's motives more, whereas my husband was so accepting that made him think all the professionals around us had Bella's best interests in their mind. He was willing to send Bella to a school with profoundly disabled children, just because the head-teacher wanted to show me the door. In a league of my own, I was thinking the local state school was just not good enough to teach my extremely talented daughter and even wished to educate her privately if only there was a private school nearby.

I was so determined to help Bella to reach her potential, I started reading everything about autism. Knowledge is truly power, it didn't simply help me to see through all the lies some of the teachers and even the health professionals said to me, it also enabled me to constantly challenge their claims which agitated them inevitably.

A year after I declined to attend the Donald Winnicott Centre to hear their verdict (having a child with developmental issues was akin to committing a crime), I was asked to bring Bella back to our GP surgery for another assessment. By then there appeared to be a brand new team being assembled in the Donald Winnicott Centre, who were not shy to accuse their predecessors for bullying mothers with children suffering from learning difficulties.

I welcomed the news, since I was worried about young mothers who might take some incompetent health professionals' advice too seriously; there are also busy working mothers with no time to question the psychotherapist's sanity nor read through all the information available to them, let alone discuss any concerns with their GPs.

It is never a good thing to get your hopes up. Bella and me went early to meet the highly regarded paediatrician from Great Ormond Street Hospital, who became the new head of the assessment team in the Donald Winnicott Centre. For all that, the assessment didn't start with a spark after the paediatrician arrived an hour late for the appointment. I tried to ignore this initial hiccup and did my best to cooperate with her by giving truthful answers to all the queries. Yet it was hard to warm up to someone who never acknowledged Bella with barely so much as a nod of the head.

After a brief dialogue with her, I felt Bella was probably better off kept busy with her puzzles, away from this dull and insipid woman. How I wished she was like my GP husband who preserved all his warmth and smile to his patients. He often high-fived those little nervous children. But the paediatrician remained unapproachable and looked like stuck in her own parallel lamentable universe. Maybe life hasn't been kind to her, otherwise how could she have looked older than her lecturer who blew her trumpet to me and calling her his best student?

While my concentration started escaping me, the paediatrician finally got round to asking me that crucial question: if Bella had any routine in her life. Naturally we humans all have routines: we get up in the morning and go to bed at night. We eat three times a day and go shopping during weekends, but I knew this was not what she intended to know.

The autistic routine is in a league of its own and hard to maintain in life, like Christopher in *The Curious Incident of the Dog in the Night-Time*, who couldn't eat his meal after the ham and broccoli in his plate got mixed together when his father angrily hit the table. In Christopher's house the furniture had to stay put - any alteration would severely impact his fragile autistic brain and disrupt his daily life or start up temper tantrums.

Bella had no such restrictions in her life, actually she is a very flexible individual. Instead of simply replying *no* I intended to tell the paediatrician an interesting anecdote to display Bella's power of adaptation. Unfortunately the paediatrician was in no mood to allow me making a little trip down the memory lane, or she simply interpreted my temporary silence as a hesitance for searching for an evasive answer to make Bella look normal and better. Rather impatiently, with a smile she reassured me that having routine is a good thing for a developing child, but I read something in her face which said the opposite.

How I wished that she didn't lie in her desperation to obtain that particular answer from me to validate her most treasured theory! Once the veil was lifted, she appeared no more respectable than the predecessor who she kept mindlessly condemning. It must be the undoing of her expertise or maybe reputation, which prompted me to not want to be part of this sham assessment anymore.

Looking unflinchingly into her eyes, something I don't remember I ever practiced before or after, and without uncertain terms, I informed her about the fact that Bella had no routine at all in her life. During my triumphant concision I noticed that she didn't just get my message but also looked awkward for being caught red-handed by someone who knew enough about her imposing intentions. Would that make her honestly entreat other worried mothers in the future? I desperately hope so.

I had no recollection of what else she asked me that day, since I stopped caring about her opinion. I turned my attention to Bella and buried my head to join her jigsaw game. I did nod or shake my head when a reply was requested, but was not too sure if they were all presented in the right order. As per usual in my life, I started drifting away from the ongoing assessment and ended up recalling the one weird parallel with the boorish psychotherapist.

At one stage I remember the psychotherapist abruptly fixed her piercing eyes on my face. Pleased that she finally halted her verbal interrogation under the full resonance, I met her gaze squarely. Predictably it upset her further, as did the lack of downcast glances from wide-eyed me. All of a sudden there was a gloomy silence since our staring match was perceived by all in the room.

Finally it was the mindful psychotherapist who ended this awkward interlude, as she likely worried that I rejoiced the dead air more. Over me, she uttered extra criticism but with less discernible effect. Reluctantly shelving her planned conclusion, the psychotherapist must have also fathomed that the fiercely protective *tiger mom* within me couldn't be tamed. I am not pushy in any sense but am ready to take a bullet for my daughter.

After I said my goodbye to the paediatrician, she came to see me twice more. Unable to summon me to the Donnald Winnicott Centre, she arrived with her team to school at a time when I was to collect Bella. We might have got on a little if only they didn't outrageously flatter me and simultaneously denounce their predecessors in a sly way.

Moreover I felt I was being stalked, since I found the entire team with Bella's head-teacher were knocking on my front door one day. Paradoxically they came to announce the *wonderful* news that Bella was finally granted 30-hours' assistance at school per week, but my signature was needed. Never having known, before, that special needs education was handed out to a competent child who had skill and talent in abundance. With numerous reasons not to sign, I denied them my signature.

Virginia Woolf wrote about *the efficiency, the organisation, the communal spirit of London* in *Mrs Dalloway*, I should think it is the glory that applies to the entire UK. With excellent governance, the state has given parents the full right to be responsible for our children's future, which enabled me to shut off any attempt of undoing Bella's progress. When her classmate with cerebral palsy only got 25 hours' assistance in a week, what did Bella need 30 hours for? We are talking about a girl who could use a fork and knife at school dinner time and was also well toilet-trained.

I saw many of Bella's classmates wet themselves and a few disrupted the class but were allowed to carry on like ferals with no one to assist or stop them. Bella quietly attended the class, following the orders as best as she could. The only problem at the time was her being unable to understand the entire instructions given by the teacher. However this problem was resolved with time; by the time Bella was in Year Two, she caught up with her peers verbally and steadfastly left all of them behind with her superb imagination which can make anything she is learning to scintillate luminously. All Bella suffered was a developmental delay, she needed more time to grow yet was never granted.

By the time Bella completed her Key Stage One SATS test with grades of 2A and 3s, one third of her classmates failed to get the required level 2 in at least one of the three subjects. Some of them failed all subjects yet a 30-hours' special needs assistance was beyond their reach. The deputy head teacher thought one needed to fight for special needs help, but why I was pestered, harassed and intimidated rather than being overlooked or ignored?

At one point the head teacher reminded me that an unruly challenge to her power could have resulted in Bella being removed from home twenty years ago. Her empty vaunt made no secret of her admiration of the bad old days, including the painful mistakes we practice no more.

I had never witnessed such desperation in anyone before, as the head teacher advised me to sign then argue with the local educational authorities afterwards. Who with a sound mind would agree for the purpose to clash? It must be her eagerness for extra money to fix some other problems at school, hence the need for me to be part of her cunning plan. But none of her aim and purpose appealed to me.

Unfortunately this was also a thorny topic at home and could never be discussed harmoniously in private. As though the pressure was not enough from Bella's school, my husband was quick to join the chorus. He found out that his many patients were unable to get the special needs help for their children who were lagging behind, which he thought I was insanely rejecting.

After witnessing so many children with short attention spans in the classroom and not achieving the required grade, I could understand why parents were marked by anguish. Without the right assistance to suit their needs, the true sufferers could never blossom in the classroom. I thought the job of a head teacher is to find joy in nourishing those struggling children and calming down worried parents. Sadly, she saw the battle of wills as the norm of human life.

It was strange to see an intelligent and highly motivated child like Bella be pursued by all these health and educational workers. An innocent explanation would be they never saw anyone like her, so clever yet verbally challenged. A sinister intention from my point of view would be for them to produce some fancier research papers to elevate their own standing.

Such aims would bear striking resemblance with John Money's, the psychologist who published many so-called research papers to announce that a child could be brought up as a boy or a girl by grown-ups' will. He used the example of a boy who lost his manhood after a botched circumcision to prove that he was already a happy girl. But when David Reimer, who was miserable all along, found out that he was actually a male, he gave up his girlish life immediately. Yet the physical and mental anguish finally drew Reimer to suicide. I think it is reasonable to question the professionals so we can protect our children from the repeat of such tragedy.

My husband's argument always was if Bella was destined not to be disabled, why not let the special needs help carry on until it became officially redundant. He was unperturbed by whether the road to announce such a redundancy might take practically forever. He seemingly was not aware of the fact that the money from the local educational authorities was never enough, hence the easily exhaustible resources should be dedicated to those children who were truly in need at this pivotal moment in their lives.

Accommodating by nature and a medical doctor by profession, my husband didn't believe that the world was devoted enough to appease everyone. That was all the more reason for me to soldier on and fight for our children's future singlehandedly, provided I could save them from suffering psychological trauma. If he didn't mind the hopeless school to claim some undeserved credit for getting Bella out of her hazy world, wait till he starts worrying when the erroneous theory becomes harder to squash.

The new speech therapist was taken aback by Bella's enthusiasm to engage in spelling with blocks while we conversed. Not many of us had found a way to instil a love of learning in the minds of our children, she admitted; which reminded me of my parents' failed efforts with my not so naturally pedantic brother. Still, schools with modern educational understanding and equipment might just be able to achieve the impossible.

During my Open University years I was taught about how to get children interested in math. Until that day, I used to think math is like Marmite, you either love it or hate it. All of a sudden, John Mason from the math department in the Open University convinced me with his innovative constructs that math can be made fun to learn for everyone.

Now Bella is thirty-one years old. She taught in the university after completing her PhD in biomathematics. She wasn't only loved by her students but also won an award for her excellent teaching techniques and effort. Four years ago she moved to work in industry as her interest is in machine learning which needs her to predict output with existing data using her extensive mathematical skills. In a world where many young women are busy to copy those bikini clad, skinny girls' act on Instagram, Bella's role model is Richard Feynman, a physics Nobel laureate.

I do meet Bella's classmates sometimes, or at least their mothers, years after our offspring are children no more, and feel sad for the failure of those once hailed by her primary school's head teacher as star pupils at that era. Education didn't seem to help them to reach their potential, let alone cultivate their relative reserves, since the teachers were so confident that some children would readily make it all the way to the top by themselves.

There was a well-known bully in Bella's school who was never taught to be friendly to her classmates. Instead, as an early speaker and precociously articulate girl, she was constantly praised for her maturity and competence. In reality, she left school at the age of 16 without even a single C-grade GCSE. So much for the blindly predicted bright future.

I always walked out from parents' meetings clenching at the long list of criticisms that Bella could do nothing right academically or socially. I also cried on the day Arthur Fowler died in EastEnders, since the head teacher refused to accept that Bella was bullied. Yet it wasn't possible to admire those mothers who were proudly parading the glowing reports of their apparently perfect children, which shockingly predicted that no improvements were ever needed for their behaviour.

Gradually it became obvious to me that for primary school teachers, children have already reached their full potential by the age of eleven - no school, university or even workplace will ever progress them in a different direction hereafter.

It was in *Emmerdale* one grumpy secondary school teacher openly expressed his relief for not having the misfortune to teach those ungrateful parents. He did seem to listen to the parents' feedback without relish. What he didn't know was in a long way he should find out that education isn't exclusively a teachers' virtue. Humans crave achievement, which is often accomplished more with the effort from nurturing parents rather than the less enthusiastic teachers during the few school hours.

There is another primary school nearby; I would intensely stare whenever I walked past it and tried to work out if its children looked any happier there. When the teacher who upset Bella a lot at Year Three was about to teach her again in Year Five, I finally decided it was time for Bella to move to that local school. It wasn't before I filed a complaint about the teacher and her unprofessional manner. I wrote in length about how she shouted at and scolded the seven-year-olds.

I never expected the widespread fear among parents, they seemed resigned to secretly bemoan about their children's misfortune rather than put their signatures to launch a successful complaint with me. One even shockingly claimed that no complaint would be upheld until a child was dead. Eighty percent of parents were unhappy that the teacher would teach their children again, but only forty percent dared to sign.

Our little hearing was hard for me to negotiate, not to mention the man who represented the Inner London Educational Authority never let the intense resentment fade from his face. That justified why most parents steered themselves clear from the complaining procedure. The shield and cover-up within the establishment was the reason that the head teacher could behave like a local mini-queen, undisputed, unchallenged, still enthroned.

Did my complaint serve as an unprecedented threat to the head teacher's reign? She remained conspicuously sullen and mortified in her effort to quell concern. Gone, too, was her arrogant and dismissive voice; with her newly improved soft image and tone of sadness, she looked vulnerable, even charming briefly. What a transformation! I left the hearing just happy Bella never had to come back to that educational setting again. Actually that was Bella's first day in her new school. It was September 10th, 2001.

*The book is the most efficient technological
instrument for learning that has ever
been devised by the human mind.*

--Northrop Frye

CHAPTER 2: READING

'Last night I dreamt I went to Manderley again.' This is my all-time favourite opening line of any book. As I like the book so much, I can never forget some lines of Daphne du Maurier's *Rebecca*, and the image of the decaying garden stayed for a long time in my head. I was a teenager when I read *Rebecca* the first time and it was in Chinese with *Butterfly Dream* as the title. But when I read it again with teenage Bella three decades later, it was not just the plot I was able to remember, much as the adjectives used to describe the plants in the garden like *vulgar* and *lanky* from the book spring back to mind.

The interpreter certainly had a lot of knowledge of England, about the Cornish coast too, otherwise it is not possible to precisely convey the mysterious and menacing atmosphere of Manderley in another language. Someone with an underlying fallacy of mythology, wasn't aware that the

Chinese *Silver River* is the equivalent of *The Milky Way* in English. In fact, he fell foolishly victim to his intuitive opinion by coining the phrase *Cow's Milky Way*, as Chinese would necessitate an adjective to indicate the source of milk. This soon became the biggest joke in Chinese literature history of translation.

Bella wasn't impressed with the film adaptation of *Rebecca.* Like all teenagers, she was more obsessed with some arresting details from the book and annoyed that they were missing. She yet had to learn that a film hasn't got the liberty when it comes to timing. For me the atmospheric description of Manderley was the tricky part for a film director to match. If Alfred Hitchcock failed to achieve it, then no one else can. Besides, the novel has become powerful because of that particular type of plant: the overgrown rhododendrons helped to intensify the mystery.

The unnamed narrator hauntingly talked about rhododendrons as 'they startled me with their crimson faces, massed one upon another in incredible profusion, showing no leaf, no twig, nothing but the slaughterous red, luscious and fantastic, unlike any rhododendron plant I had ever seen before'. I believe Alfred Hitchcock did his best to present us with the type of rich and vibrant rhododendrons Du Maurier described here at a black and white film era. At least he didn't miss any necessary storyline and managed to cast Joan

Fontaine as Maxim's beautiful young bride which certainly satisfied me and a lot of the filmgoers as the alter ego of the nameless narrator out of the acclaimed book.

Nothing could please you more than seeing your child learn to read. I don't have many memories of reading bedtime stories for Bella, since most of the stories we had ever discussed were all read by herself. Yes, Bella had started reading before she started talking. When she was barely four, her nursery teacher found her playing on her own while talking to herself too. He settled next to her quietly and found Bella was reciting the entire story of *The Very Hungry Caterpillar.*

He was awestruck that Bella didn't get any details wrong, retelling the whole trajectory of the caterpillar to butterfly process, including what the caterpillar ate on each day of the week. In effect I was impressed too, since Bella suddenly progressed from reading word by word to fluent sentences. Why should I read to her, she reads to me and always followed by our lengthy discussion. I think we spent more time talking about the stories rather than reading.

Language is humanity, that is what Noam Chomsky said before he waded into all types of political arguments. I certainly took Chomsky's definition too seriously and started my first line in my first ever TMA (tutor marked assignment) at Open University as 'Babies become humanised through the process of learning'. Obviously the tutor got very concerned, she corrected me by saying that babies are humans from birth, and through learning they become social creatures.

I know some of the psychologists would disagree with the tutor too, since they would say that becoming social is innate for humans, others may argue that babies are born with empty mind to be shaped by experience later. Chomsky also claimed that children must have an inborn faculty for language acquisition. I initially believed that the neural circuits containing linguistic information were faulty in Bella's brain at birth, now I know that there is never such a hardware in our brain to start with.

What I learnt gradually is that fortunately there are many pathways in our brain, if one is blocked it is possible to utilize the spare ones there. Bella is active in constructing her own learning like most of the children, not a reluctant learner like those children who truly suffer from autism or crippled by other types of learning disability. That was why I rejected all those fatalistic suggestions from the so-called specialists and confidently carried on talking and reading with Bella.

The end result did indicate that Bella's language developmental delay could be thwarted with consistent stimulation. At the later stage, the head teacher who tried to impose outrageously long hours assistance to Bella did sulkily admit that the special needs support could make subsequently complacent parents halt their own consistent effort in helping the children.

Nevertheless against the backdrop of all the misunderstanding, I for one instinctively felt that Bella could only progress with a double dose of education: home and school. Talking late left a lot to desire for Bella's natural interaction with her classmates on an equal footing - as a result I had to leave it to the school to conductively advance Bella's less than satisfactory communicational skills.

Sadly the self-centred school's solution was very often irrelevant, futile and could be caustic at times, the same way like their lack of insight to many other children's acute problems too. As a matter of fact, it was impossible to have any gainful discussions with the head teacher before Bella was officially declared as normal.

Without the comfort of hindsight, it was a mighty hard task to deal with the obnoxious cynicism from those assessment personnel in the Donald Winnicott Centre. Most of them seemed to hold the behaviourist views with children as passive receivers of experience, as a result they often blamed the rearing environment delaying children's maturation.

They also speculated that the lack of emotional connection between the so-called *refrigerator mothers* and their babies was the source of children's development failure, and were more or less recklessly telling mothers that they were deservedly suffering from their own deed by not spending any time with infants.

Presumably these so-called child development experts are not aware of the fact that human babies are so vulnerable and need years of caring to be alive. No mother in the world would be cold, stupid and lazy enough to sit down there to watch their babies work out how to walk and talk one day all by themselves. I think the great poet William Blake had described this divine connection between mothers and their children most eloquently in 'On Another's Sorrow': *Can a mother sit and hear/An infant groan, an infant fear?/ No, no! Never can it be!/Never, never can it be!*

Hein Rudolph Shaffer was a renowned child psychologist. He was evacuated to England as a young Jewish boy from Germany where his parents later died in the concentration camp. His life experiences helped him to choose his career as a child developmental psychologist. While working on attachment theory, he found out through his research that Japanese mothers don't really talk to their babies. Instead of bonding with newborns as we are encouraged to do here, the Japanese believe that newborns are bonded too much to mothers already at birth.

To help the children to become independent

individuals in the future, they prefer to keep a distance which includes not talking to them during babyhood. We are all aware of the Japanese as a vocal and creative nation and don't associate them with any language developmental issue. Surrounded by a language environment is enough for babies to acquire speech. Some might need extra help like Bella, but most can manage by observing, playing and communicating for their daily needs with parents.

One of the ethnic groups in Xinjiang is called Xibo, they are more like the Han Chinese and Manchurians, but with their own tongue. They could only claim a shared history of two hundred years in my homeland and Uyghurs call them Shiwa, it means ten children in Mandarin. My father recalled the tale of how they came to existence which started in the 19th century, when the ruling Qing government confined ten newborns in a prison-like environment. These babies were fed by prison guards silently – in fact the prison guards were categorically forbidden to converse with each other in front of these babies.

The moral of the story is that the babies invented their own language and that is what their descendants speak in the present day Xinjiang. Along with this fake language developmental fable was the Qing authorities' resolute endeavour to cover up the fact that they brought the Xibos in from the far East Heilongjiang province to control Uyghurs in Xinjiang. Xibos were also used as masonries to fight the Dungan Revolt and the Russian occupation in many harrowing decades to come.

Heilongjiang means *black dragon river* in Chinese. It is the Manchurian homeland in the northeast of China, 3000 miles away from Xinjiang so Xibos could not keep up their attempt to escape back home on their own. Born in Xinjiang, I was brought up in the capital of the Heilongjiang province, Harbin, so am indeed well aware of the vast distance between the two areas in an era when one can rely on trains to travel there. But the deception of improvised connection seems inexhaustibly sufficient for a lot of Uyghurs to accept this entirely different ethnic group as indigenous people of Xinjiang, not realising that a language doesn't get invented in a couple of years by ten babies.

My only knowledge of Xibo was a famous film director from this ethnic group, she kept producing Uyghur films based on the Han Chinese tradition. In her film about Nasreddin Hoja, the witty Uzbek legend caught the king who was clumsily trying to climb through a window to get into a pretty maid's living quarter. Uyghur kings could legally marry four wives, so why would he go through all this unnecessary predicament and subsequent humiliation!

You don't expect a Xibo to understand Uyghur

culture, yet she was endorsed by the authorities financially which enabled her to produce many culturally inappropriate movies. It prompted a Han Chinese journalist to question on newspaper why a story about our legendary Nasreddin Hoja wasn't welcomed by Uyghurs!

I thought the way schools teach reading is meant to give children a taste of good things to come, but was disappointed to see that teachers sent everyone back home weekly with a little book about Biff and Chip's activities during Bella's reception class years. It is an Oxford book series, telling about a simple family life with only a few pages to flip through.

Each book took mere minutes to finish, but Bella read the books with me over and over again, instantaneously the teacher was alarmed that Bella could recite the entire book. In reality anyone with a reasonable memory would remember all the words just by skimming lightly through those lines. But the teacher thought Bella lost her focus and failed to understand the plot. She also claimed that all her classmates had a good grasp of the stories.

If it was true then why years later a boy from the same class was classified as unable to read at all? His mother was furious that her son had slipped through the net until he was in Year Five already. It took six teachers to discover he had a serious learning difficulty. All those wasted years and missed opportunities must have exacerbated his troubles further. Possibly after spending all their time keeping up with Bella's seemingly enigmatic life, the teachers might have lost sight of their other duties.

Anyway we literally stopped reading those little books more than just once, so if Bella ever needed to look between truly concentrating and attentively responding to the teacher's questions, she did then. Luckily early during her second year in that school, Bella finally got some fun books to read and with one that stayed in our mind after all these years. By then pupils were already grouped up by their capacity, and as a competent reader Bella was in top group with a book by Christian Andersen.

I love the story of *Ugly Duckling*, it transported me back to my cherished childhood and what I constantly told Bella that she was truly a swan in making. But this book had only got Christian Andersen's plot but written with someone else's less-than-impressive wording. A long page was dedicated to the surrounding of that river before the mother duck finally appeared on the next page. I don't know how other children from the group enjoyed it, but we found it hard to get through. Bella's lack of enthusiasm made the teacher swiftly downgrade her to the next group, then she was given one of the most entertaining children's books we had ever read. It was Sandy Toksvig's

Unusual Day.

On a school unusual day, a girl brought in a clover with five leaves, another child brought in his baby brother's dry nappy he wore all night as it was supposed to be wet in the morning. Jessica brought in her granny who the teacher had to send back home with an apology that granny would be welcome during the school's Family Day. Jessica was upset since grandma was very unusual, she had not taken up knitting like other old women but was always active and jogging daily.

Unable to concentrate, Jessica looked out from the school window and found the building opposite was engulfed by fire. Soon the fire engine arrived and the teacher took the entire class out to watch how the fire brigade put out the fire. Disturbingly someone was trapped in the top floor and crying for help, as a result a firefighter climbed up the ladder to bring down the old woman who cuddled up to her cat on his back.

When they were safe on the ground and the firefighter took off her helmet, everyone cheered to see that she was Jessica's grandmother. Now the teacher had to apologise again and telling the granny that she was absolutely unusual. Nevertheless Jessica disagreed, for her grandma was only unusual because she could spin plates with both hands.

With an amusingly exciting storyline, this book

helped six-year-olds to enjoy and comprehend the true meaning of the word *unusual*. Bella and me talked about it during mealtime so often and induced my curious husband to read the book too. After he learnt the plot, my husband told Bella that it was very unusual to be able to spin the plates using both hands, which I considered an utterly improbable interpretation of the book. He discarded all that vivid description of an older woman being a firefighter and uncharacteristically climbing up the tall ladders to bring another adult down on her back.

I asked my husband who happened to be in his fifties then if he could rescue someone down from that height, he simply replied that his GP's duties didn't include such activities, but shockingly insisted that it wasn't unusual for older women to join the fire brigade. And he must have generally assumed they all volunteered to climb up the high building when many young male firefighters were idling down below.

The argument went on and there seemed no way for us to reconcile our difference, for a closure we looked at Bella to be the judge and finally she gave her verdict: Jessica had an unusual granny. As a further boost to me, her like-minded mother, Bella agreed that spinning plates has no value in life unless one is working in a circus to entertain the crowd. Jessica's grandma was an exceptionally brave and rare old firefighter, Bella concluded.

Bella spent her last two primary school years in the school across the street after leaving the one down the road. She had a wonderful time there. There was a bullying incident soon after she started new school which she reported to her teacher immediately. The teacher took action and the three girls didn't only apologize to Bella, they also started playing with her. This certainly is the school that has achieved its educational goals for every single child, unlike the previous school Bella attended which always sided with bullies and left the weak ones to fend for themselves.

By the time Bella started Year 6 in primary education, we learnt that her previous school ridiculously formed a booster class in the evening to help the capable pupils to up their game. In contrast, the new school Bella was attending aimed to bring up the standard for the entire school population. The head teacher proudly declared that all pupils should reach level four on science in the SATS this year, just like they did the year before.

Finally my faith in education is restored. It was sheer bad luck that the first head teacher I had to deal with was totally overbearing, unpleasant and unprofessional but finally I am convinced that she was also a one-off. A bad fish could never be able to spoil the whole pond. On one occasion she reprimand me with a sneer for expecting Bella to be happy in her school. It was not long before she brought her son to be taught in her own school with the excuse that he was unhappy somewhere else.

I took Bella out of that school after getting fed up with listening to her preaching, which she never practiced herself. No doubt, I ultimately found the school for Bella to be happily educated. When I look back at my life, I consider this as the best decision I have ever made, since I had unfailingly provided Bella the opportunity to be merry and bright in a fine school. I still read the glowing report Bella had received from her teacher before she went to secondary school, it stated Bella as 'a unique child, highly intelligent and extremely likable'. That is Bella alright and finally the school got it.

Bella certainly got the three Ms, that is memory, math and music, just the first school she attended wouldn't accept it. They did call her a mathematical wizard (a true title for girls should be witch; maybe that is why most girls hate math, simply to avoid being the holder of that horrendous title). Perhaps it was not a nickname given to flatter Bella, but chosen to fit perfectly well with their autistic definition.

Furthermore, they tried to convince me that Bella couldn't do art. According to Bella's teacher in Reception class, she had to stop Bella short before her paintings were complete, as she didn't think Bella had enough imagination to fill the paper. I wondered what Bella could have produced if the school bade her to rise with her creation, and had to settle with encouraging my disheartened daughter to indulge in her artistic fantasy at home.

Therefore it was a sheer surprise when I learnt that Bella is an exceptionally talented artist during my first parents' meeting in her secondary school. Bella was already eleven years old, now with immeasurable pleasure I found out that her other classmates typically started learning composition whereas Bella was already painting as good as a sixteen-year-old.

I sent Bella to a local girls' secondary school, as my big sister highly recommended that to me after spending her six teenage years in the only girls' school of Harbin. I never expected to have so much fun during Bella's GCSE years when I voluntarily started doing English Language and Literature alongside Bella.

That was the first time I was introduced to John Steinbeck, the unquestionably deserving Nobel laureate. Hanging onto my rejuvenated enthusiasm, I went on to read *The Wrath of Grapes* by Steinbeck after I studied his *Of Mice and Man* with youthful Bella. These books gave me a panoramic view about the Great Depression in 1930s America. They were exclusively about ordinary people's lives during that period, the variety of people that life had dealt a bad hand with, be they disabled, black or everyday white American folks.

Even the books I read before Bella started her GCSE, like Charles Dickens' *Great Expectations* and Shakespeare's *Romeo and Juliet*, had to be mused over in a good light through a thorough analysis. Details I had missed on my own reading were now being highlighted, like Magwitch was sentenced to death with no less than another thirty convicts, not unlike the mass execution in some of the human rights-violating countries these days.

All that suffering must be tragically endured with stoicism and possibly alongside hope by Victorians. Our apparently less than polished past allowed me to be cautiously optimistic in a still very unpleasant world with sustained violent resolution to conflict. In spite of that, my ponderous heart is struggling to expect that all countries in our world will find a passionate way to wipe out the barbarism of capital punishment soon.

School is a playground for children who ride high in science and don't sink in literacy too. Bella found parallel strategies in studying maths and English Literature, for her it was all about proving that you aren't wrong. Essay writing is a useful tool to discover how one can identify the author's message lurking between the lines, and Bella was always able to unearth the hidden truth then articulate her alternative perspective with her mathematical precision. That was also the TMA writing era of my Open University years, Bella thought I approached it like going to court to defend myself with sufficient evidence.

It was the wise, brave and determined Juliet Bella earnestly pitched against the equally romantic but apparently more feminine Romeo. For her the way Juliet committed suicide was more masculine in comparison to Romeo's poisonous ending. With ample evidence from the book to back up her claim, Bella convinced the teacher to grant her the top grade. The way Bella did her literature research wasn't dissimilar from the thorough and rigorous manner she approached her mathematical formulae.

After studying *Great Expectations*, Bella was surprised that Magwitch has not turned into a household name like Miss Havisham (stands for the embittered woman, disappointed in love and withdrawn from the world), but for Bella he is certainly one of Dickens' most memorable personae. She thought by disclosing Magwitch's inner life to the readers, Dickens successfully created a character with a very compelling development.

Bella told me while following Magwitch's rocky path to self-awareness, she has experienced an emotional rollercoaster: from hate to pity, from suspicion to perplexion, from concern to admiration and from love to respect. Magwitch is the man Bella was scared and wanted to get rid of in Chapter 1 of the book for the safety of little Pip, but eventually also becomes the man she found difficult to let go of when she put the book down. Such is the mighty power of Dickens' words.

Bella's essay was described as mature sometimes, that could only be the unintended consequence of my input from our extensive discussions, as I wasn't sure how far I should go in helping her. Not until the handshake from Bella's all-time favourite teacher, Miss Emerick, gave me the encouragement and much-needed approval. She thanked me for helping Bella to produce the excellent piece of *Medieval Medicine* coursework, which certainly kept me busy ordering all the reference books from Amazon then reading as well as analysing with Bella.

When Bella was asked to write about her favourite book, she talked about *The Secret Diary of Adrian Mole, Aged 13 ¾*. She told her teacher that Sue Townsend produced a gripping novel with her amusing slice-of-life descriptions, which is more a view of mine that Bella agreed with. We did watch the TV adaptation of *Cappuccino Years* from Sue Townsend later, as always Bella wasn't impressed with the cast and found the small screen adaptation not loyal enough to the original writing.

As someone with an overactive imagination, I tend to get disappointed by my favourite characters on the screen. I know directors are allowed to interpret the books as they please and very often leave their marks there by altering some of the details as well as the ending. In *The Count of Monte Cristo* Alexandra Dumas let the protagonist Edmond Dantes succeeded as an avenger, but his forgiveness didn't extend to the scope to take his childhood sweetheart back.

Contrariwise some adaptation did allow him to remain in that little village of France with the first love of his life. Hope prevailed here but not as the book concluded, where Dantes sailed away to the Orient to begin a new life with his tested new lover. *All human wisdom is contained in these two words: 'Wait and Hope'.* This final foresight might have propelled some directors to engage the audience with their own innovative ending, but certainly dissatisfied those who loyally applauded the great author's authentic closure.

During my Open University year I was taught that learning to read is an interactive and highly complex process. To read we have to utilize our phonological and linguistic skills to grasp the purpose of the text. It goes without saying that reading is a language-based skill, some poor readers are also sufferers from specific language impairments with restricted vocabulary or weakness in grammar. But as a less-studied disorder, it is not clear if these poor comprehenders' oral language deficiency is the result of their limited reading practice or the cause of it.

Other poor readers seem to be unable to decode (pronounce the written word) at an age-appropriate level. Coupled with good comprehension skills, these are typically dyslexic sufferers, yet still are being considered as typically developing children without impairment for many years.

The head teachers from Bella's first primary school lamented me as ungrateful for all my refusal for having her labelled. She thought I should connect instantly with worried parents and be thrilled to jump the long queue. I feel for those parents, all asking the special needs assistance for sound reasons, but seemed to have come to a wall. Amidst a backdrop of pursuing their own unjustifiable agenda, how could school find enough money to support children who are lagging positively behind! No wonder so many adolescents take their leave from school without qualifications and disillusioned, never fit to earn a living.

Despite their true capacity in learning as Jean Piaget discovered, now we know that children learn to read by being taught. It was Russian psychologist Lev Vygotsky who alerted the world that learning isn't the result of children's solitary effort. Vygotsky emphasized the aspect of children as social beings, and considered their cognitive development essentially as a social process. For Vygotsky culture is the most important ingredient in children's intellectual development. He emphasized the fact that learning occurs when children interact with more competent others (parent, teacher or peers) from their own community.

Of all the cultural tools, Vygotsky regarded language as the most important one: through the development of language, children's interpersonal communication will reach a new height. The internalisation of language will help children to develop their thought and improve their understanding. Unlike Piaget, who cannily called self-talk *egocentric speech*, Vygotsky aptly named it as *externalised thought*. He subsequently pointed out its crucial role in helping children to clear their minds when engaged in problem solving.

I discovered Vygotsky long before I entered Open University, during my bewildering years of Bella's delayed development. I was plagued with worries that Bella would never be able to string a few words into a meaningful sentence. Apart from living in fear that Bella may never be able to enjoy an independent life in full, I was also frustrated with all the criticism around me as an incompetent mother.

Albeit did I never believe that motherhood can be pinned down by a definition, as my children's precious formative years were ticking away, I decided to confront the storm by *learning to dance in the rain*. I embarked on a journey to get a piece of formidable scholars' mind from my trusted books, so that I could practice any sensible advice which might benefit Bella.

The first time I walked towards the psychology section in a nearby bookshop, I was shocked to see only books like *Men Are from Mars*, *Women Are from Venus* were on display there. 'You call this psychology?' I mumbled to myself. After a long search, I bought a book introducing Sigmund Freud and found him dealing with children's emotions only, but not cognitive development.

It was in our local library I came across John B Watson, the vocal proponent of the scientific theory of behaviourism. 'Give me a dozen healthy infants, well-formed' he said, then he boasted about his ability to train them to become any type of specialist. It was his last intensely thought-provoking statement that stuck in my memory lastingly: 'I am going beyond my facts I admit, but so have the advocates of the contrary and they have been doing it for many thousands of years'.

I think deep inside we humans are all behaviourists, like the psychologist Anna Freud, the daughter of Sigmund Freud admitted once upon a time. So we have been advancing our children's intellectual development for thousands of years without acknowledging it, or realising. Only with children like Bella, the exercise becomes a conscious effort. Children are all born with dreams, that little person is also yearning for success, big or small and that is what I always see in Bella.

Despite her initial inability, I could see her ambition, the desire to achieve, merely falling short of the means to get there. My worried husband had started asking his patients how they dealt with their children's language developmental problem. One shocking remedy he discovered was not to offer children food or drink until they utter that word. I was horrified and told my husband that I would prefer a mute child to a starving one. Something I live to regret, since Bella might have come out triumphantly as a much on-demand scientist, but Esin, my younger daughter who is well fed, physically fit and beautiful but also unfortunately a mute 29-year-old adult today.

Looking for an answer, I dipped into the book the domineering psychotherapist I met in the Donald Winnicott Centre ordered me to read. I still remember the vainglory in her zealous gaze when she handed the book to me, supposedly my life problems are all included and could be solved by that booklet. The author claims that everything we do can affect our babies from the moment they are conceived, but which are the positive effects and how to avoid the negative ones are not specified.

I intently studied the book, genuinely read it

twice yet was not any wiser. I felt like sitting on a plane with an incompetent pilot circling the runway forever, the concrete answer never took off the ground. By then I have two daughters already and with a tubal ligation, so why I would need a hazy to-do or not to-do list for future pregnancies, a book I wouldn't recommend to an expectant mother in a hurry.

I probably was only six years old, when my excited big sister one day came back from school to claim that there was a book which had the answer to all our life problems, it is called *One Hundred Thousand Whys*. My parents went to the bookshop with her and finally the whole family gathered in the sitting room ready to kiss goodbye to all the troubles in life. Rukiye, my eleven-year-old sister, started by reading and translating into perfectly comprehensible Uyghur the reason why we need to sleep at night, and went further to say that no matter how much we nap during the day we still couldn't make up the night sleep we may have lost.

Father wasn't convinced, he had to get up at 3am to feed and milk the cows in the farm, and always had his afternoon nap to make up for the loss of sleep from the small hours in the morning. With a newly sharpened understanding, Rukiye reiterated the uncanny argument from the book that a man with a ninety-year lifespan shouldn't spend sixty years working and the remaining thirty years sleeping. 'What a nonsense' was

Father's instinctive refutation, and he did go on to live 91 fantastic years with the help of his nap.

There was some urgent issues Father desperately needed an answer for. In the extreme cold of the Harbin winter, our water pipes would be frozen and leave us without water supply, which was a true hazard for our farm because of the lack of the gallons of drinking water for cows. "How could we sort this problem?" he asked. With immense desire to help, Rukiye swiftly found the page for the frozen pipe and started stating the obvious through her reading. Of course it is the cold Harbin weather to blame, it could go down to as low as minus 30 degrees Celsius, but the book stopped short of offering a remedy. Father got up and left, so did Mother, but not before telling Rukiye her book was not what it claimed to be.

Soon only Rukiye and me were left there, as the curious me solidly anticipated all things written as stories and pressed Rukiye to read on. According to Mother I virtually spent an whole year pestering Rukiye to read the entire book to me but always to no avail. In reality this was only volume one, with many more to follow in the bookshop which never managed to make their way to our home. Two years later when I finally racked up enough Chinese words to read this big book myself, I stopped blaming Rukiye for all her refusal, since even the communist propaganda book *How The Steel Was Tempered* was a far more interesting read than those endless *whys*.

So early on I already had a taste of the fact that life's problems cannot be sorted by clear gain, if any, from a single book only, let alone about an issue as complex as child development. In retrospect, I am not surprised that someone wrote a book about making babies. By doing so the author initiated the issue, drew attention and inspired discussions. No book can be considered as useless, precisely like no theory in psychology is perfect before endless debates to further our understanding. It was misleading for the psychotherapist to pass the book round like a Bible to fazed mothers who could do with an answer or at least some assistance.

As the frantic effort of trying to fix me rather than helping Bella disheartened me, the acme of offence only rolled in when the tactless head teacher asked me if I felt guilty for having disabled children, as if I had certain control during the natural selection of my genes! I felt fortunate to have two beautiful daughters long before I knew Bella will be a high achiever, and it is Esin who makes me always proud.

Though profoundly disabled, it is her who taught me about unconditional love. Like a source of light, Esin helped me to catch the glimpse of heaven in our family life, consequently she also enabled me to appreciate the fact that children are a pure blessing rather than someone to fulfil our expectations.

Only later I understood the Freudian psychotherapists simply wouldn't accept any valid theory in child development. For them all humans are miserable creatures, and the true happiness will finally appear when we start owning up to our *calamitous* past. She must be even fuming that Sigmund Freud's theory is not included in the psychology curriculum of all universities in the world. The truth is developmental psychology has come a long way from the time of John Locke, the great English philosopher who considered the child's mind as a *blank state* to be scribed by experience.

Opposite to John Locke's empiricism there are also philosophers who see children as merely mini adults who are born with innate ideas which will mature into fullness all by themselves. Now we are aware that children are naturally curious, willing learners and capable of making sense of the world with efforts. It is Piaget's constructivism which gave prominence to children's active involvement in their intellectual development.

But Piaget considered children as largely independent agents interacting with objects only. It was Vygotsky who pointed out that children live in a social setting and swiftly learning about their own cultural interpretation of the world from adults around them. Ever so resourceful, Vygotsky focused on children's potential and suggested that under adult guidance children can be elevated from where they currently are to where they aspire to be. He called it the *zone of proximal development*.

With astonishing insight and an illustrious career, Vygotsky came up with all these valid theories before the age of 37 when he died of tuberculosis. He studied law in the university, had a critical sense of an artist, but became influential in the research of the relationship between mind and society. The way he described the process of maturation and subsequently children's language development stood out brilliantly in cognitive psychology.

The behaviourists had their roaring 60s after Skinner taught the pigeons to play ping-pong, but had to turn to Piaget's constructivism in the 70s to count on children's solo aptness. Vygotsky was rediscovered in the 80s long after he was left out of educational psychology. His social constructivism combined the best part of the environmental factor with children's endeavour, which means relying equally on collaborative means as well as the youngsters' active quest for knowledge.

During my short encounter with the overreacting psychotherapist, who constantly reminded me of the grumpy Mr McGregor from Beatrix Potter's *Peter Rabbit*, she also found time to order me to stop teaching Bella. She vilified my claim for educating children as hopeless, and was in much pain to insist that as a basic principle one should only play with them. She probably imagined that Bella was forced to sit behind a desk in her bedroom staring at the blackboard fixed on the wall.

The psychotherapist, in my opinion, may not be a mother herself, since she wasn't aware that education at home is purely a natural event during our conversation at play time, tea time, shopping trips as well as holiday excursions. I was elated to see Bella started untangling fact from fiction which belonged to her tender years, and when she accepted that Santa Claus and the Tooth Fairy are mythical childhood characters, that means learning has happened.

I eagerly measured all those tiny steps of progress in Bella's behaviour and was satisfied when Bella's teacher in Year Six claimed that she was a pleasure to teach. Contrary to the learning disabilities wildly exaggerated by her first school, Bella was a good problem solver. What I noticed from the way she approached problem solving was that the knowledge she once grasped was not just stored in her memory but also being enriched. That is the only way for me to explain why once Bella started talking at the age of five, she suddenly progressed so fast and bypassed any other child in her spheres.

When Bella was four the time was ripe to teach her spelling and she learned the word *umbrella*. A few days later when she saw the words Union Jack in another book and loudly read out 'onion jack', she then proudly waited for my simultaneous compliment to be paid to her masterly pronunciation. It may seem comical, but it also highlighted the fact that Bella had already grasped that one sound of the letter, u, and was not shy to apply it generally.

That probably was the beginning of schools starting to teach children to say the alphabet with its sound rather than their names, but I saw no such need. After all Bella could generalise, could remember the exceptions (like learnt to say Union Jack accurately). Not to associate each vowel of the alphabet with a particular sound could be the best head start to handle the not so rule-abiding English words smoothly, unerringly and swimmingly in the future.

For me life is a problem-solving process, why not concentrate on something more important rather than the sound of a set of weightless letters! Reading is like a breeze if all you have to do is to combine characters from the alphabet - trying to memorise each Chinese word was a far bigger challenge I had to face during my early school years. But the hurdle wasn't for long either, soon all of us were reading with different degrees of fluency, at the same time some never learned how to do math.

During a teddy bear tea party, my friend teased Bella that she was left without a spoon to stir the sugar in her tea which Bella pretentiously put on her saucer. Unable to find a spoon, an unfazed Bella rapidly picked up a toy mouse instead. She then cheekily offered to stir the tea with its tail. The funny incident stayed in my friend's memory for many years to come, but this made me aware of Bella's agile capacity in solving all her problems playfully, resourcefully, also unfailingly.

It was in the same year I conducted the famous Sally-Anne test to see if Bella had *Theory of mind*. The test is devised to reveal if a child is suffering from autism by finding out if she can read other people's minds, that is what *Theory of mind* is about. I let the doll called Sally put the marbles in her basket, then moved Sally to the other room. During Sally's absence, the doll called Anne shifted the marbles into a box. Now I brought Sally back and asked Bella where she would look for her marbles, Bella pointed to the box. Children with *Theory of mind* know that Sally would look at her basket first.

When I told my husband about the result, he went pale and worried that Bella was suffering from autism. Not so fast, Mr.! I reminded him that only 75% of normal children can get the answer right. Bella could well be among the 25% of those with the wrong answer. Besides Bella probably thought I asked her to help Sally find her marbles. With Bella's limited verbal communicational skill, she was unable to clarify the question with me at that time.

I personally failed the test recently if my husband cared to remember, a normal forty-year-old mother of two, with university degrees and years of teaching experience. When my husband asked me where *should* Sally look for her marbles, I told him the box and could only say Sally looked at the basket first if he asked me where Sally *would* look for her marbles when she came back.

During a lunch break in the Open University I talked about my failed Sally-Anne test to my classmates for a laugh, but was surprised to find out from one teacher that many of her primary school colleagues were also unable to pass the test. It seems that when questioned wrongly, the Sally-Anne test has less to do with the *Theory of mind* than turning into a simple farce.

No wonder many psychologists criticised Piaget for underestimating children's deduction skills from his conservation tasks, as they thought children likely misconceived him. With plenty of room left to ponder Piaget's tests by using alternative wording, in the years to come, many psychologists are able to discover that children can look at things from other people's view at the age as early as four, not seven as Piaget claimed. We know now that at least half of the three-year-olds are aware of the fact that Sally hasn't got a clue that her marbles are moved.

Much of what Piaget's experiments which he used to access children's cognitive competence are problem solving tasks, because problem solving involves learning rules and discovering strategies, and strategies are pertinent to most aspects of cognitive development. Take problem solving by *trial and error* as an example, children have to use their memory to keep track of which strategies they have tried already, otherwise it could take them too long or be unable to solve it.

Some more complicated tasks need children to plan their move and identify sub-goals, and many children can achieve the overall goal by thinking in this sophisticated manner. When it comes to the cognitively less demanding *hill climbing* approach, children need to select the correct strategies at first, otherwise it will be impossible to overcome the obstacle and to get close to the solution.

By focusing on that all-important source of intellectual development of children, Piaget once famously declared that 'Freud chose emotions, I chose intelligence'. Piaget's approach gained a devoted and enthusiastic following in psychology. Some may criticize him for neglecting children's feelings, nonetheless find it hard to deny the fact that every problem solved brings novel understanding to children with cognitive advancements.

Reading is also a form of problem-solving process since reading is not just about speed and accuracy, its ultimate purpose is to achieve comprehension. Because at the centre of all reading is the aim to extract meaning and information from printed text. To obtain meaning-based representations of the text, children with inference generation skills can make links between individual sentences and paragraphs to establish coherence. They also understand sentences like '*if the cat doesn't eat the food, throw it away*' where *it* refers to food, not the cat.

Watching Bella to read, I always notice that she tends to reread some sentences for clarification. And when we discuss the stories, she always linked the reading to her prior knowledge. I have gone through all the books Bella read until she started her university degree. We talked about the plot, the moral of the stories instead of my asking her why, when and where. We often concluded that these books have become popular because they closely reflect true life events. Even *Harry Potter* is about friendship and loyalty, albeit happening in a faraway fantasy land.

During Bella's GCSE years, the English literature teacher asked the class to read the story book *Face* together. Each girl was supposed to read one paragraph, and when it was Bella's turn, gone was the lacklustre and hesitant utterance of some readers and in came Bella's fluent narration plus the different tone she had adopted for each character.

Seeing a plain reading had turned into a fun performance, the class cheered and pleaded the teacher to allow Bella carry on reading the entire book alone without interruption, as if they could go back to their childhood and enjoy listening to their favourite bedtime story in the classroom. I was over the moon to hear her articulate classmates, who are fluent at chit-chat and started talking probably four years before Bella, then looked up at Bella eerily, like she were a mother figure.

Bella's first primary school tried hard to play down her other strengths by claiming Bella is only a mathematical genius to fortify their autistic definition attempt despite her often writing excellent essays during her time there. An entertaining and informative essay Bella wrote at Year Four was passed around in school for other teachers and children to read. I obtained a copy too and found Bella convincingly talked about the invention of music and why humans started wearing shoes.

I was amazed by Bella's description as well as her imagination until a year later I found the same story in a *Sesame Street* episode. I know it was not a small feat to retell the story with such clarity and using her own words, but Bella must acknowledge the origin of the narrative at the beginning of her writing. Bella was nine years old to learn the word plagiarism and the appropriate punishment to follow suit from me. Isn't that what home education is about, progressively guiding your children out of their ignorance!

When Bella got the top score for her speaking and listening in secondary school, she told me the teacher commented about her all-meaningful eye contact with her audience, namely her classmates at that time. I asked Bella about the rest of her classmates' performance during their turn, she comically told me some looked down at their feet for the entire period. One kept playing with her fingers and another one would interrupt her speech from time to time to ask for permission to sit down. All were denied by the teacher.

There were girls who filled up their speech with *Oh* and *Um* to the teacher's dismay, which they were clearly instructed not to include in their speech, not to mention the pauses and loss of words for the others. So these girls, vocal from the age of one year onward, still found it hard to articulate the simple events during their recent two weeks' work experience. When something so simple only mastered by so few, you realise that instead of teaching those young *souls to fly* like William Blake demanded, school left the adolescents to leave the educational settings unable to walk and talk.

Now looking back at Bella's education, the only credit I can take is I taught her to read, and the rest she achieved all by herself. During Year Ten, she happily told me that when the teacher asked if anyone one had read *Jane Eyre*, she was the only pupil who could proudly lift her hand in her class. Apart from literature, art can too be learnt through reading, which I found out accidentally.

As someone who frequently struggled to produce a decent art homework in my school years, I was always in awe of those classmates who were able to present beautiful paintings to be displayed on the school walls. Without much of the gifted artistic gene in my body, I bought a book for Bella about how to draw when she was six years old. Bella was taken to it immediately and soon started drawing portraits for everyone she knew. At a time when the British nation was fascinated by the BBC's *Walking with Dinosaurs* series, Bella started drawing all different types of dinosaurs.

Upon examination of her painting, I started realising Bella's eye to detail, especially the obvious details I have always missed, like the different types of antennas on the Teletubbies' heads. I started understanding the source of my artistic limitations, but more proud that I helped Bella to reach her potential by encouraging her to read. If motherhood is about unleashing our offspring's potential, in my own way I have achieved that.

As I am admiring Bella's easy sailing in her life and career with a sense of fulfilment, I also cannot hide the disappointment of failing to help my younger daughter out of her silent world. I did everything required of me with all my might, but failed to start off the songs and maybe symphony within Esin.

I never planned to replicate the same success like Bella's while bringing up Esin. I know she is destined towards a quieter and more complacent existence, as a result could have been just as satisfied and contented to live a simple, as long as an independent life. Though even a life like that is elusive for her forever. Esin is a happy adult, but lives a life solely depending on me as her full-time carer.

In the book of life, the answers are not in the back.

--Charles M. Schultz

CHAPTER 3: ESIN

Esin was born normally, without forceps. Her face was wrinkled with birthmarks and her eyes seemed squashed. When I was leaving the hospital next day, the nurse who captured the sight of Bella with her father expressed her surprise that how different my two daughters looked.

Not quite! In a month, as if by magic, the birthmark became paler and until it finally disappeared, Esin's wrinkly skin became as smooth as any baby's and her eyes got bigger too, as a result years later people kept considering my daughters as twins. Unexpectedly, my husband was also guilty of confusing their baby photos with one another, but for me Esin has her father's Mediterranean looks whereas Bella is more Central Asian like me.

For me the biggest difference is in their characters: Bella is an eager beaver, on the other hand Esin is carefree and easy. Giving the impression that she felt intimidated by her knowledgeable big sister's unflinching courage and formidable energy, Esin tends to settle for defeat before realising there could be a victory in sight. All those promising signs of looking deep into our eyes and moving her lips when she heard spoken words surprisingly came to nothing.

I feel like talking about another life of Esin's, when she was able to count to ten comfortably. It definitely was before her second birthday. She did try to count from eleven onward, but that became blunderingly illegible to everyone else except me. Sadly all that has been irrevocably ended and she never managed to call me mummy either.

Even before talking, Bella was able to follow instructions, but not Esin. There is very little she can understand and frequently relied on context, such as lunch time, teatime or bedtime to guess her next step. I always tell people life is a series of surprises for Esin, as she rarely knows what is going to happen next. As a result, save for my determined efforts to adjust everything for Esin's pleasurable purpose, normally on any day, but unfortunately not without occasional mishap.

When Esin was six years old, we took Esin on her first holiday abroad with a suitcase stuffed with her favourite toys and snacks rather than nappies. Esin finally completed her toilet training then, when later in school her teacher commended to it as a great achievement, I had to reveal that Esin did it all by herself. It was like one night she took in the divine sign then the next morning got up to live her life nappy free.

The chartered flight left from Heathrow at night, so Esin was entirely unaware that we were flying, and only realised that we travelled by air on our return from Bodrum, Turkey. Esin screamed as the plane soared against the morning sky, luckily it was drowned by the deafening sound of the plane taking off to have other passengers disturbed. I held her hand and kissed her, but what really calmed her down was when she found no one else panicking, at the same time she herself wasn't swung out of her seat. So there is some type of reasoning within her, it seeks out the rational which guided her to enjoy the rest of her journey.

By the time the local educational authority found a suitable school for Esin, she was already seven years old. Tyssen is a community primary mainstream school, and that year they set up an autistic unit to deal with children who were suffering from learning disabilities. It is not possible not to feel hugely grateful for all the teachers who had taught Esin in their efforts to improve her chance in life.

Esin's charms radiated through all those artful plays she had to take part in, especially the one she had to come out finally as the beautiful swan. The teacher helped the tutu-wearing Esin to spin on stage, which she did admirably with a smile. Therefore Esin became very popular in the school; children were pleased to see her in the supermarket and at the Science Museum. After greeting Esin they would introduce themselves as her schoolmates.

When I was asked about Esin's progress as she had completed her first academic term in the school, I hastily replied none. I could see how disappointed the teacher was and soon realised my mistake as I invariably set the benchmark for Esin's development against Bella's pace. The underlying argument from the teacher grew clearer when she revealed that Esin started walking in a straight line and could also look up at the teacher when her name was called during the register.

So learning has an entirely different meaning for Esin. Everything has to be broken down into tiny, tractable pieces. They may seem minuscule but can be considered as an achievement, if, say, Esin merely sat quietly with the entire school in the assembly hours. Later, during my years in the Open University, I was made aware of the fact that learning is a change in behaviour which can be sustained, hence by that definition Esin is learning every day at her own pace.

Gradually I stopped expecting Esin to communicate verbally. Sign language and Makaton stickers would have been viable communicational alternatives; unfortunately Esin never managed to crack any of them either. Though my coming to terms with Esin's impairment wasn't that straightforward. Until

Esin was eight years old, I lived with the combination of dread and desire, of despair and dream. In the morning I always eagerly greeted Esin, to see if she started miraculously answering back, and went to bed with the renewed hope by reminding myself *tomorrow is another day*.

Then, one night, Esin died in my nightmare. I only managed to stop crying when I found Esin was peacefully sleeping in her own bed. Looking at her beautiful face, I finally acknowledged that God has given me an amiable and pretty girl in all fairness. Esin is pleasant, funny, mischievous and caring in her own way, what more can a mother expect from her child in the real world.

Esin is impatient, just like the young me. Though the hardship in life has left me without any choice but to accept that *patience is a virtue*, Esin on the other hand is luckily spared of the agony from waiting for things to happen. Esin can afford not to wait, as she can get me running by a glance, and order her desired meal from me in a flash. During her Tyssen school years, teachers would ask the children to set up the table for morning tea in pairs. The wonderful training may have taught Esin about sharing food and responsibilities, it also inevitably left Esin in pain to see her partner at work without an identical memory like hers.

The chore could be a minefield for some to work out the owners of each cup, but for the purpose of enjoying the tea sooner, Esin often briskly grabbed the cup from her confused partner's hand and placed it in front of the rightful heir. Having her midmorning snack was Esin's great pleasure - she wouldn't allow her classmate's hesitation to delay it from happening.

People always ask me how I communicate with Esin - it is mainly guesswork. Luckily I am familiar with almost every single shade of her desires, and consequently have been helping Esin to pursue reality akin to her thoughts on daily basis. I have diligently turned myself to one of those mothers who knows best, because Esin is unable to tell me what she wants, what she really, really wants. There is a smart allusion in this line to an Uyghur proverb, which claims that a *mother understands her mute and deaf child's tongue.*

Besides, Esin is capable of delivering all her potential feeling to me with a variety of her smiles. She has this grateful smile to tell me that I have come to her timely rescue, like the moment I had offered her a bottle of water when we were out on a warm day. Along with her good nature, Esin is a pleasure to be with. My life isn't plagued with the constant obligation to deal with her temper tantrums, only those occasionally sad and quiet moments to consider. And there is nothing a glass of water or a piece of Esin's favourite Parmesan cheese can't fix.

Recently we met a young woman near Clissold Leisure Centre when I took Esin out for walking.

She came to greet Esin excitedly and introduced herself as Nicole. I couldn't believe she is that other girl in Tyssen Primary School Autism Unit with Esin years ago. She is now a beautiful and confident-looking young woman, far from her relatively destructive and unvalued past. She seemed to exercise regularly in the leisure centre. She told me she was about to start a new job next week.

Mush as I was very pleased to see her living an independent life, a few flashbacks unfolded her very different junior years. It is hard to link this charming and sensibly-talking woman to that little girl who once needed so much attention from teachers to stay calm during her Tyssen school days.

Nicole is always articulate. During one of their school trips to a leisure centre outside London, I couldn't help overhearing her talking to the boy who had already left Tyssen School but came back to join us for the day out. They had a lot of catching up to do. At one stage the boy disagreeably told Nicole 'go to hell'; Nicole anxiously replied that she wouldn't go there. The boy then explained to her it was just a way to declare his opposition, Nicole refuted again: 'I know what you mean, but I don't want go to hell'.

It is not possible to remain indifferent when listening of children who suffer from autism freely expressing themselves vocally. While cherishing that amusing and perfectly compelling moment, one can't stop wondering what is ultimately hidden beneath such a disorder.

I tried to tell the boy that I watched him on TV, but he seemed more embarrassed rather than delighted to converse with me. No wonder some people consider autism as an extreme shyness. It was an hour-long program on Channel Four, mostly about his life. I learnt that he was a Star Wars fan, and knew everything about the plot as well as the characters in the film. He had a huge collection of Star War memorabilia and his father, not a wealthy man apparently, seemed to do his best to help his son to indulge in his hobby.

The boy also dealt with the moment about his mother's tragic death from cancer on TV. The recollection must have been too traumatic to express, since his mother already died during the time he and his father were struggling to reach the hospital in the rush hour traffic. With unceasing pain, he hid in a box to narrate the entire event. I had more pleasant memories of him during his Tyssen school days, when he saw Bella joined them in a swimming lesson the first time, then promptly shouted out: 'Two Esins'.

Esin obviously didn't recognise Nicole, how could she? Even I needed Nicole to come forward and introduce herself to me. We able-bodied people have many ways to extend our memories: spoken words, written diaries and photo albums, only to name a few. I have memories of Nicole's own way to show her fondness to Esin during their primary school years, but Esin was always wary of her tight hug and probably hated the wet kisses too.

I had witnessed Esin hiding behind me when she saw Nicole was marching towards her, and had to gently remind Nicole that Esin didn't enjoy kissing as she did. Then Nicole tried tenderly holding Esin's hands, though Esin stubbornly succeeded in making it clear that she would rather hold my hands instead.

Sixteen years has passed since Esin and Nicole had parted their ways to go to secondary school, and never again will they share the same platform with their markedly different abilities. But something remained same, that is Nicole's abundance of love for Esin could be sensed throughout. I can see it from her sparkling eyes. What a lovely girl!

Autism is always portrayed as a mind-blindness and being aloof to human feelings, but all I can see from these children and young adults around me is nothing but love. Who said they couldn't read others' minds? Take Esin for example - she always carefully examines my facial expression for approval. After finally becoming a proud owner of a face plastered with smiles, I wonder if Esin has wondrously touched my emoticon button early on. No more lost in deep thoughts for me, as it can be interpreted by her as dismay. If speechless

Esin can gain consent by analysing my facial expressions, then all the others can achieve that too.

I don't know why we often ended up discussing *theory of mind* when traveling in the car. As those debates raged on with endless *I know*, *you know*, I tended to raise my voice in my attempt to convince my husband and sometimes Bella too, though she mostly agrees with me. Unable to follow the argument, Esin often anxiously squeezed my hand, which would compel me to lower my voice or terminate the discussion. The last thing we want is to have Esin worried, she needs my delightful exterior to survive.

Autism is reduced to a few lines of a checklist and given to primary school teachers, which granted them an undeserved attitude of well-trained experts. Believing life was that simple, a barely 20-year-old teaching assistant contemptuously lectured me on the importance of fearing the worst during Bella's primary school years. The young woman didn't understand that *fear is a pair of handcuffs on your soul* but not a remedy for the condition. I would accept the special needs help if it was tailored to address the problems rather than heedlessly labelling the child.

Bella was shunned by her classmates during her early school years when she was desperately in need to develop her social interaction skills. It would be a great assistance from school if other children were encouraged to play with her, but Bella was bullied and as always, my complaints were neither investigated nor tolerated. I moved Bella to a different school and it breathed a new life into her growth. If Bella ever intends to write a memoir in her life, I will suggest that she skip her vanished unpleasant days before Year Five.

I learnt to swim at the age of 45, something the young me was unable to master despite growing up in a city with the famous Songhua River. My fear of water instantaneously became trivial when I realised Esin could drop out of my grasp, and my sight if I couldn't venture past the shallow water. Marvellously, I started floating above the not very calm waves. I went far beyond my capacity to guide Esin not to cross the safety net or swim into uncharted territory.

By the time I had decided to go to Open University to study child development, I was also prompted by the desire to help Esin better. Being over fifty years old was not my concern at all, not least because I was spared the misfortune to rely on reading glasses to study my textbooks. Although the education was a rewarding and fun experience, it invariably left me with more questions rather than answers for Esin's condition.

The head of the department of psychology in Open University was a diehard behaviourist at that time. I still remember Kiran presented us with Ivan Pavlov's portrait and gushed about 'great man, great beard'. Like most people, I was aware of Pavlovian Classical Conditioning and heard of how he used stimuli to entice salivation in dogs. His discovery of the relationship between environmental stimuli and consequent behaviour responses had triggered a degree of modification in classroom disciplines for better academic outcomes.

My first assignment in the OU was to assess the four grand theories in child development. I could pinpoint the difference between Pavlov and Skinner's *behaviourism* with Piaget and Vygotsky's *constructivism* easily, but Bandura's *social learning* theory left me unable to decide which camp he belongs to. Finally I declared Bandura, similar to Piaget and Vygotsky, was placing children's active participation at the heart of learning and development. The tutor marked me down; she commented that Bandura was a behaviourist - she even went so far as to say Kiran should never have elevated Bandura to an exclusive category of his own.

Bandura is famous with his *Bobo doll* experiment where children imitated the violent behaviour. That evidence was used by parents and teachers to decry the violence on TV as the source for ever-growing adolescents' crime. Kiran was not wrong to consider Bandura to be in a league of his own, since his *observational learning* experiment does give children an active role in basic form of learning. Though imitation can't go far enough to directly lead to problem solving, it definitely can make children think and comprehend reality.

When visual material is used for teaching, like the *Bobo doll*, children find it easier to get involved and the consequence remains vividly in their memories. (Bandura did include the clips where the violent participants were punished later for their crime). No wonder Bandura has become such an influential psychologist and his social learning theory is considered to be bordering *behaviourism* and *constructivism* in child development.

The Behaviourists did triumph in taking care of those children who can't or wouldn't actively construct their own learning. The ABA (applied behaviour analysis) technique is based on *operant conditioning* by encouraging autistic children to utter the words one by one, which sometimes does set them forward to reclaim their rightful place in our verbally communicative planet. I have seen a child being taught intensively for many hours a day, and awarded with his favourite drink when he repeated the word, for him progressively to gain his speech.

I am still wondering if Esin could have acquired language with the same teaching technique. I went to a Makaton course, and the teacher claimed that they got children talking in two weeks after lengthy daily coaching. I wanted to enrol Esin to the training but was told nine-year-old Esin was not young enough for them. Accordingly after eight-years of age, these mute children already accumulated so many bad habits, it wasn't possible to implement the divine Makaton plan anymore.

When a valuable intervention like this became ungainful because of its inextricable connection with age, it felt surreal in the form of rejection. Was that too great an opportunity to miss or is Esin simply untrainable? This is one of life's questions, or maybe delusions; sadly, I would never be able to find the answer.

Esin never had a brain scan, so I am not sure if there is some abnormality there, although many papers I have read always claim that no difference can be detected between autistic and perfectly functional brains. A neighbour's seemingly normal-looking grandson was diagnosed with Asperger's syndrome. He was articulate in an echolalia way, and everyone commented about his sheer brightness, yet his countenance took on a dull expression as I tried to converse with him.

He also ignored a girl's repeated call unsociably and carried on playing his own game by showing no curiosity beyond the realm of his own existence. But if he wanted to engage with you, he would go out of his way enthusiastically and charmingly. His Russian mother took him to Moscow for a brain scan, and was nonchalantly told that one side of his brain was more developed than the other side. The implications of this unequal development wasn't explained, and a remedy wasn't offered either.

I watched him to leave his secondary special education with no qualifications. He now lives in a care home but is able to explore London streets on his own safely and get back to rest there at night. Compared to him Nicole's story is a developmental success, while she looked a lot less promising to start with.

Do people grow out of autism? Nicole looks like any young woman of her age - not a trace of abnormality can be seen during our short encounter. After all, our social interaction and judgement about others are all based on this kind of superficial contact. Only the person we are married to can create a shock wave to our system with some odd behaviour we never detected before.

Most of us can find a way to start sharing the same sense of proportion in our marriage, but it is also the marriage that informs us that *we boil at different degrees*. Though psychologists, with infallible authority, tend to group us up for what we have got in common as human beings and single out those traces might require their attention, or labelling. Anyway, Nicole is adorable, no matter what anyone in her close affinity may whisper discretely to my ear about her.

The question I do want an answer for is whether Nicole was autistic to start with. Autism is a syndrome, like a gigantic umbrella covering a lot of abnormalities. From a scale of one to a hundred, we can all easily fit into somewhere, and men are supposedly more autistic than women. I think this is a way to declare that men are less social than women, or less talkative.

As always the only female engineer among a group of male ones, I found men also enjoy gossiping as much as women, what they don't do is express their feelings, at least not in public. But I don't think that is what autism is about. Far from it, it is a disorder on a grievous level. For me the tragedy is that the sufferers of autism live in a parallel universe, as a consequence they lack the skill to take care of themselves independently in their lives. Strangely this allowed some people to claim that our world isn't autism friendly. In addition some doctors are focusing on those capable individuals with autism rather than the vulnerable ones.

As a GP, my husband always attended medical conferences, and at one stage he came back excitedly to tell me about an autistic woman who addressed hundreds of GPs. The woman was young, articulate and seemed very convincing about her account of autistic life, as a consequence my husband declared that he got more insight into this syndrome. What I gathered from him was that the young woman was functional, actually at the higher end of human intelligence, so I wondered what was failing her to be declared mentally handicapped. The answer was not much.

The woman claimed that once her car was broken down on motorway, so she started behaving strangely until the AA arrived to rescue her. "What was her strange behaviour?", I pressed on and I was told she started flapping her hands. Is that all? Facing a crisis like that in a no man's land on our own, most of us might do more than just flapping our hands to keep calm. Should not we leave this accomplished woman alone and concentrate on assisting those disabled helpless people?

It is widely claimed that autism is always accompanied by higher intelligence or extraordinary skills. I think the film *Rain Man* did a good job to contribute to this misunderstanding. Dustin Hoffman's character was at least able to make some money from a casino using his feats of memory and deduction ability until he was kicked out from there, but others are unable to put their fragmented skills to any good use.

At a time when you can click a keyboard button on your laptop to uncover any given date between 1880 and 1950, what is the use of remembering it like one of the most studied autistic men *L* did in his life? Life problems are solved by linking our knowledge to the current situation, whilst autistic knowledge is *scattered like shells on Egyptian sands.*

They are unable to put their mastery together for any practical purposes, regardless of years of expert help.

It reminds me of my university days. Once, I was frustrated by failing to solve the last exam question and asked a classmate how he handled it successfully afterwards. He enlightened me with the technique we recently acquired, which was overlooked by me during my tense exam hours.

As all exams are meant to teach you in the most unforgettable way, I learnt to go through all the options in my head before giving up in the future, which isn't limited to my exams only. Or put it another way, to link more than I had ever done before in my life.

I have been observing people who are excellent in their jobs and successful in their studies for years, and noticed they are all good in linking their knowledge from different fields. Luckily there is no shortage of candidates for me to study, Bella and her clever PhD colleagues all seem to possess this type of complex skills. On the other extreme, when I examine Esin's classmates, I can see the opposite.

From watching Esin alone that much I could identify her willingness in giving up, let alone give time for the neurons to link up inside her brain for problem solving. Symbolism is considered to be the stepping stone for language development, and that is where autism fails spectacularly. The sort of act like riding on a broom as a pretend horse is never a game for children suffering from autism to play. They fail to make the link.

Language is arbitrary, so are all the writings in the world. Our resourceful ancestors recognized the importance of communication, and found ways to attach meaning to words symbolically with thousands of different languages all over the world. Of all the spoken languages I am aware of, I can only see Chinese is embroidered with meaning. The word sun might be a rectangle now, but initially was a circle with a dot. The moon is a word in the shape of a crescent whereas the word cry has a tear squishing out from the corner of your left eye. And particularly because of these meanings, the Chinese language is laborious to learn, it takes years to memorise the combinations of those lines and dots.

Meanwhile, the rest of the world simply chooses to create all the consequential words by combining of a few dozens of characters in an alphabet. This complicated system called language, with grammar as its rules, is understood by the toddlers, at a time when a lot of them just have managed to walk. At the age of eighteen months old, children are already conversing and engaging in pretend play.

When Bella failed to develop her speech at the age of two, my mother on the other side of the world blamed me for speaking English to Bella. Mother thought Bella could've started talking a long time ago had I communicated with her in Uyghur, since it is an easier language. Though her idea was laughed at by my husband and me at that time, the suggestion made perfect sense to Mother, someone who only spoke Uyghur fluently and never managed to speak Chinese or Russian in the same manner.

Because of our environment, living among Russian migrants in a Chinese city called Harbin, Mother needed both languages to survive there. Admirably, Mother understood far more than she could express, and always double-checked my interpretation during those young and immature years of mine.

Compared to Mother, Father was able to express himself much better in Chinese or Russian, but could rarely fathom what was said to him. I believe his vocal competence came from his desire to be in the thick of the conversation, while Mother may have thought it hardly worth it to draw additional ridicule.

One day a Han Chinese visitor needed a bottle to store milk from our farm and was not sure if the empty bottle Father found for him in the shed was hygienic enough for the purpose. He expressed his fear that the bottle was ever used to keep poison, but the word poison was beyond Father's comprehension in Chinese. Looking at Father's perplexed face, the visitor helpfully added that he meant the liquid one uses to kill the mice.

There was no way Father could miss the word mice, the little vermin causing so much mayhem in our farm. Immensely shocked, Father exclaimed: 'What do you need mice for?' It had passed the point for me to take no part in the amusing exchange from the next room. I stepped in to advise the visitor to wash the bottle and assured him that it was always used for milk storage.

The way Father understood just one word from the sentence reminds me of how children initially can only pick up the noun or verbs from adults' speech. Language development is very similar to learning a second language; which one is harder I am not sure. Despite the fact that not everyone can manage a foreign tongue, most children progress to fluent speakers in their native tongue.

Now linguists reject the idea that we need special hardware in our brains to learn to speak, but they still struggle to explain why autistic children fail to develop speech. The way autism affects brain development is not the same like language impairment, they see the world differently and miss most of the cues we communicate through our facial expressions. They can never catch their own light from other people's eyes.

Remarkably Esin is a mind reader. She would go

into withdrawal if she found me with a stern or even thoughtful face, otherwise she can joyfully misbehave when I am smiling, especially laughing. As someone who was born with a serious expression as my resting face, I have substituted it with a smiley one, any other way would hinder Esin's happiness. Befittingly, my forties has become the decade of my transformation, I have learnt to swim and managed to plaster on a smile or laughter to my now agreeable face, all for Esin's sake.

Esin's approachable and pleasant demeanour tends to appeal to strangers, who always ask her for directions when we are out for a walk. I am wholly happy to answer on behalf of Esin, as I also have to concede that no adjustment can turn me into someone as likable as her. Additionally I am still wondering if Esin is suffering from autism, since Esin's survival seems to purely depend on my emotions, which is far from the definition of autism.

Time and again I read that people are delighted to be diagnosed with autism, since they can finally pinpoint the reason for their odd behaviour. Before Esin was ten years old, once my husband put a poster from the NHS on the fridge door, which had the images of some autistic behaviour. Soon I found out from BBC children's news that a little boy diagnosed himself as autistic by studying this poster. His mother happily declared now the school couldn't call her son naughty anymore, they had to provide special needs assistance for his studies instead.

There was a clip of him on TV walking behind his mother, staring on the ground and apparently talking to himself continuously. He looked autistic alright, and I am surprised his symptoms were sloppily missed by the teachers, who are always well-trained to spot any sign of abnormalities. School is an institution specialised in squeezing some extra money out of the local educational budget to feast on their own agenda.

Suddenly autism has become so straightforward to diagnose, now people started labelling each other autistic. Moreover I can recall that the author and commentator Toby Young once published an essay to reject being called autistic. It was after his wife wrote an article about his behaviour on national newspaper, someone then pertinaciously asked Toby Young to be left alone as he was apparently autistic. The amateur diagnosis from the stranger was spawned from a vignette that Toby Young took the nanny to attend a film premiere with him when his pregnant wife was unwilling to come. He was seen as insensitive to his wife's feelings.

Toby Young explained that only his brother is truly autistic, since it takes a great effort for him to go from A to B - even getting into a car is apparently a struggle for him. I happen to agree with him. As an Oxford University graduate, Toby Young's bounty in life includes a Hollywood film about his time in America. The movie *How To Lose Friends & Alienate People* gave us an eyeful of his unsocial impulses, yet he returned to Britain with a beautiful wife and now the happy couple is blessed with a few children too.

It is people like Esin and Toby Young's brother, who lack a flexible mind and creative imagination that deserve our attention. These people's survival purely depend on others and are unable to survive in this world for a single day on their own. Mild forms of autism can even be a driving force for success, and there is no shortage of candidates to take them up as partners.

Teaching autistic people is still a work in progress, as some of the consequences brought about by learning can unbelievably undo their barely existing worldly skills. Like Red, after he was released from prison in *Shawshank Redemption*, Esin started ridiculously waiting for permission to enter the bathroom. If this is how an emphasis on complacency leaves Esin detrimentally in discomfort, I would rather she returns to her early, spontaneous, unschooled days. It isn't the lack of inner impulse from autism stopping Esin from significant advancement, any more than trying to instil some common sense in her.

I used to participate in a workforce survey once a year. It was about qualifications and our jobs; I think the government intends to trace the change over the years as we advance. The surveyor must have been intrigued by the disparity in the ability of our family members. The fact that Esin isn't just without any degrees as qualification, she is also unable to speak, read or write is a rare phenomenon.

During the first interview the surveyor tried to clarify if Esin was suffering from learning difficulties or learning disabilities, and it was the first time I was compelled to do some serious thinking about the difference between these two learning alignments. As humans, many of us suffer from some types of learning difficulties, but not many people, maybe only few in a teeming population have to live with learning disabilities in their entire lifetime, with devastating consequences.

When I was growing up, dyspraxia was unheard of which I probably suffered from for the first two decades in my life. I was a clumsy child, would apparently trip and fall on any visible block from my path which for some reason everyone else could see except me. I had no communicational problems then, not when I was talking to one person only, but in a group chat my opinions were rarely taken up and people used to talk over me.

In my late teens, I started trying to fix my problems and discovered two deficits in my communicational skills; one was not having eye contact with people who I was talking to and the second one was not taking turns during group chat. After much trial and error, I finally mastered the art of eye contact. It is not about staring without blinking until you are tired to the point of being unable to utter your speech, but the technique is in delivering an attention worthy eye contact when you are making a point.

After my big sister Rukiye went back to Urumqi to teach in Xinjiang Technological College, we made a tape and sent it to her together with the newly bought recorder. The recording auspiciously begun after Mother asked us to say our message, but upon listening to the taped message when the recording was over, I was shocked by my inability to take turns. I kept intercepting when others were talking and not speaking properly when it was my own chance.

Petrified by my ill manners, I looked at the others and instantly realised that blame rarely came children's way from my loving parents. But even my brother and little sister were all smiles, not at all offended by my objectionable disruption. Never again I doubted the love from family, though it also undeniably blinded us from our numerous shortcomings in life.

Many years have passed since I threw a well-prepared message into disarray, but it taught me to bite my lower lip hard to bar the urge to interrupt, and to only respond when I get a look of request for my opinion. Though talking less, suddenly I had noticed that my idea mattered in group chats. Strangely, silence enabled me to be heard.

After the age of fifteen, I didn't only stop falling by paying extra attention when I walked, I even started wearing high heels without a shred of struggle. Always dwarfed by others with my five foot one inch frame, I was ecstatic that those much-needed few inches could be attained with elevated shoes.

I wasn't upset that God has been mean with me vertically, since I am blessed with a mathematical brain in a time when it was the sole criterion for intelligence. Clumsiness aside, I was always hailed as this clever girl in primary and secondary schools, which I enjoyed smugly. It was in my university years when surrounded by many brighter future engineers, I then grudgingly conceded that the top spot of the class couldn't be mine anymore. Still teetering in high heels, I duly comforted myself that at least I could hide the fact I am short forever.

It was during that time I read an essay written by the foreign minister of the Philippines. Adam Malik was apparently short on height but a high achiever diplomatically, he was chosen to be the President of the UN General Assembly in 1970s. He talked about his vain young years wearing heels to disguise his shortness, but realised he was defined by his brain and finally ditched his padded shoes.

In one of the heated debates of UN, he concluded his speech by saying that it was the duty of us dwarves to fight against the giant bears in the world. He was having a dig on the then Russian ambassador, since he did stare at the direction of Russia at the end of his speech.

I seriously admired his individuality and was aware of the many tales of small countries that resisted and fought back invasions of large countries, like Finland fought Russia with Molotov and won in the 1930s. Be that as it may, I still haven't found the courage to walk on flat shoes. With my not so sensible, even debatable fashion sense, I may well be buried with my heels one day.

Thirty percent of people who were born with dyspraxia finally grow out of it, as I did. Thirty percent will get worse and live a disabled life. The other forty percent of sufferers will remain as they are and live with some type of learning difficulties forever.

My increased mental fitness through overcoming dyspraxia is not directly the result of myself actively embarking on a journey to copy the behaviour of the normal folks around me, it was just not that severe to start with. It is like those dyslexic TV personalities and politicians can strive in their job unfailingly by merely paying additional attention to what they read. Because their learning difficulties never started from the disabling end of the spectrum.

On the other hand, Esin's disability is thrust upon her on a quite different scale - at the age of 29 she still remains at a toddler's level in most of her understanding, though not without a faint flavour of notably mature insight as well. Nonetheless it is the immature act of hers that defines Esin.

Once, on the upper deck of a bus, Esin stepped on a passenger's foot. It was partly the passenger to blame, as she left her feet in the aisle instead of keeping them safely under the seat in front of her. To defuse the matter, I immediately apologized to the woman, so we all could carry on with our journey peacefully. But the woman was still fuming, and not at all satisfied with an apology somehow. Pointing to Esin she expressed her desire to hear Esin personally apologize to her.

How was Esin going to do that, and why couldn't she see Esin's disability! Esin walked past her without looking down at her feet which was obvious to all of us there. As the woman was voicing her ridiculous demand, Esin remained in her seat, and righteously, with an air of detachment from her surroundings as always. As far as I was concerned, the matter was already settled, and the only way to keep our journey quite was to give this insensitive woman a complete brush-off.

When I completed my first year in primary school, one of my classmates was not allowed to progress to the next year with the rest of us. During dinner time I expressed my concern about my classmate's fate. Mother, who once taught in primary school, told me that it was obligatory to pass the end-of-year exam to enter the year ahead. 'What if he never passes?' I asked anxiously, since I noticed he could neither read properly nor solve math problems.

My big sister talked about her once classmate who was stuck in year one for five years, as if to justify his towering height among the eight-year-olds. No form of disposition could survive such a bitter experience; no wonder those traumatized children would gradually drop out from school with their grade one qualification only. Luckily the world has moved on from that cruel time and Esin was allowed to enter secondary school at the age of eleven.

Ickburgh is a school for disabled children only. Some of the students were so severely disabled, such as paralysed from the neck down. It was a humbling experience to see these children are wheeled in, yet unquestionably accepting and smiling throughout the day. Soon after Esin started her school, the death of a pupil was announced in a newsletter. It was heart-breaking to know that such a young life had perished, and maybe a painful life all along.

It didn't take long for the school to find out that Esin was far less abled than they initially anticipated, as she ignored all their instructions.

Whereas other children might be shorter than Esin or with less symmetrical facial features, they had no problem to follow the orders. Esin was fittingly placed within a group of children more like herself, and a dedicated teacher, Peter, took them to Tate Museum everyday driving a minibus himself. I happen to believe that Esin has some exceptional insight to lift her understanding of the meaning behind those ethereal art works.

Esin was a year old when we took her to Brighton. She stopped crying with the glimpse of the sea, which she submitted herself to humbly ever since. She was more than just delighted, in fact she stared straight ahead almost without blinking her eyes. Maybe imagination took the reins, and prompted Esin to pay homage to the orderly nature and reality in front of her.

During our holiday in Bodrum, we never missed a day at the sea to view the manifestation of the spectacular sunset. In the fullness of time we also kept our long gazes locked on the dark and turbulent waves to comply with Esin's silent and gratifying hours. In 2004, a few months before my father's death, my mind had drifted through my cherished childhood memory and reverie with the ebb and flow of the moonlit sea. Since then I would see my father riding away from me in the celestial current, further and further to a realm forever beyond my reach.

It was during one of my thoughtful moments

at the seaside, I finally reconciled with the fact that all types of language were now beyond Esin's reach, since she was a teenager already. Puberty is used as a cut-off point for fluent language development. Children who study a foreign language before this time can speak the language without an accent, which becomes impossible afterwards. That is why I was desperate to see Esin talking before the age of eleven.

Now I wouldn't mind if Esin speaks with an accent, or slower than most of us, as long as she can communicate her desires. With too many life skills to attain, I value the one making your likes and dislikes clear the most, and it could have helped me to guide Esin to embark a career for her pleasure and satisfaction. What a dreamer I was way down and deep inside. So the futile dreams are composed during the day with hoarded longings of mine, I confess. The nocturnal dreams help us to relax, to vent our fury and alarm us about the upcoming complexity in life. Mother was right to give them so much thought, I can see why she was always the wise one.

CHAPTER 4:
ATTACHMENT

It is accepted wisdom that infants need years of care to mature physically and psychologically, but only the Open University taught me that the close bond between the parents and their offspring is equally crucial, which is theorised as the growth of attachment. Now most of us are aware of the fact that the prolonged period of childhood does not just provide survival opportunity for human infants, it is also a crucial time for them to learn from their parents and caregivers.

There seems to be no shortage of successful people who have a strong attachment with their parents, people who could benefit from the accomplishments of the previous generation to advance their own actions. That probably was the reason why the psychotherapist in the Donald Winnicott Centre was so desperate to alter the narrative of my happy childhood. She needed a sad story from that time-capsule of mine to complete her theory, which inextricably connects my two daughters' developmental issues with my past; alas a lost world had to be buried under layers of troubled dust to satisfy her.

Once upon a time, the behaviourist's modern fairy tale deluded us into thinking that babies only needed a soft blanket instead of mother's warm bosom to mature. Sooner than expected, psychologists were horrified to witness those baby monkeys who were brought up with milk bottle and soft toys become wholly cold mothers to their own offspring. These orphaned monkeys never knew how mothers took care of new-borns, as a consequence they wanted categorically to have nothing to do with their own brood. That was when mothers' presence as a passionate carer and an undisputable role model became evident in child development.

Bonding seems an instinct for humankind as well as an animal need. The story that the goslings bonded with Lorenz (the psychologist) and followed him everywhere, explains why the ugly duckling attached to the mother duck as soon as it hatched. It was a mix up of the eggs, for the cygnet ended up with ducklings, yet the heart-warming part of the story was the mother duck truly cared about her conspicuously odd-looking baby all the same. The relentless cruelty towards the cygnet was from the other ducklings, who were still learning about the complex world they just entered and had yet to understand the essence of love and tolerance.

After John Bowlby first alarmed the world about the significance of the mother-infant relationship in 1940s, the research into attachment finally took off twenty years later. Mary Ainsworth constructively introduced the procedure that was called *Strange Situation* to assess the attachment between mother and baby. The test separates mothers from their infants for a short time then analyses the reaction of the babies towards their mothers once they are reunited.

Infants who felt uneasy when mother left but become very happy once she reappeared are those securely attached to mothers. The insecure type often don't respond to mothers' attempt of contact once separation is ended, and worse for some to be so angry and that they cry when being picked up then crying more when placed back down.

Following up these infants into their mid-childhood, the researcher found that the securely attached babies generally grow into confident and popular children in school, meanwhile the insecure ones would become prone to aggression later in their lives or become attention seekers inimitably.

It is all very well to come out with an effective theory like this to measure how children are able to regulate their emotional state in the future, but I always wonder how much infants' inborn temperamental characteristics were taken into consideration. I have three siblings, and frequently remember my parents talked about how they were endlessly entertained by some of us while finding the others so off-putting or even annoying, in particular.

Parenthood is never about leaving your children entirely to fend for themselves, but being encouraged by an easy-going child can be an added bonus. Those happy, unequal traits can carry children triumphantly through to a popular adulthood and encourage them to embrace a gratifying future.

Since Bowlby always emphasized that attachment is a lifelong phenomenon, various attempts have been made to find empirical evidence to support the claim through adult attachment interviews. The interview, by its design, is to elicit the participant's early childhood memories of attachment in which they found themselves, and is always done by looking at how participants feel and reflect once plunged back into their childhood background.

What is said would not cause a stir, as the way they say it or how they evaluate those experiences is the particular focus on the impact from their past. According to the coherence and emotional openness of the participants, some psychologists discovered three distinctive patterns out of them, the classification is to correspond with the three types of childhood attachment.

A securely attached child will give an autonomous narrative as an adult. These mature, competent adults are able to give a comprehensive account of their early relationship with their parents objectively, they also acknowledge the importance of these relationships to themselves and the influence they have in their lives.

The insecure-avoidant attachment is related to dismissive adolescents, who are usually in denial of their past attachment history, particularly negative parts. These hostile and friendless adults are more susceptible to adversity and stress because they consider personal relationships with little significance and are unwilling to acknowledge its influence on themselves now.

The third group is classified as preoccupied adults, who are pronouncedly considered to be the most vulnerable ones and can be conveniently likened to the ambivalently attached children. Their narrative is usually emotive, they seem to accept the influence of their early attachment in their adult life, but are confused or failed to resolve the issue even after the termination of the past. *Neurotic patterns can be seen originating here* as well as their anxiety in social circumstances.

The way men are unwilling to talk about their feelings can easily place them in the insecurely attached category by mistake. For example, my husband never talked about his childhood. From the fragments I could gather during our decades-long conversations, I could see nothing unpleasant might have happened. My parents-in-law were caring enough and looked like no unresolved issues after all. With a touch of dismissiveness to my curiosity, my husband always answered 'we just did what a normal family do', which could give psychotherapists the impression that he was avoiding discussing some painful events in his childhood.

Probably knowingly our Donald Winnicott psychotherapist pursued someone weightier like me for guaranteed substance. Had my bored stiff husband excelled himself to declare a life of total detachment, he may have caused barely a ripple to those who disregard the paternal influence. That was why I found it strange when the Open University offered us a video with three men willingly talking about their early attachment history, until I realised they were all actors and the video was particularly produced for us to write our attachment TMA informatively.

Bowlby could be right when he claimed that attachment between parents and their infants have an evolutionary base and biological function to guarantee survival. According to him this early relationship between the infants and their caregivers has a significant influence in their future development, because in the course of relating to their attachment figures, the infants start building up a set of expectations of their own ability to get help.

These expectations include the availability of the attachment figures when they need them, as well as the outcome of the communication between them. Bowlby called this mental representation *internal working models* (IWMs) which is useful in assisting the infant to approach new situations with confidence. According to Bowlby, once IWMs are formed, it serves as a prototype for all other social relationships children form in the future. This includes their mid-childhood, adolescence and adulthood.

We lived in an uncharacteristically large garden for an urban setting in Harbin. As the only Uyghur family there we felt a dog could keep us company and chase out the belligerent intruders, that was when Yolvas (means tiger in Uyghur) joined us. Yolvas was only two weeks old and looked more like a piglet rather than the ginger coloured German Shepherd he had grown into later. I used to watch Yolvas sleep when he was a cub, and felt sad to see he kept shrieking in his apparent nightmare, as if he was chased by a real tiger.

Even in my early teens I was aware it was separation anxiety from leaving the comfort of his mother's cuddle and breastfeeding too early. He enjoyed his decade-long life with us but was strangely timid for a canine of his size, especially during the rowdy Chinese New Year Eve fireworks. I cannot forget the way he fearfully buried his head in the pile of hay in our back yard farm.

It usually was a sleepless night for me, and certainly for the frightfully scared Yolvas in the kitchen. How I wished we could endure the inescapable explosions in my bedroom together, but was worried I might offend Pasha, our privileged cat, who always shared my bed and condescendingly considered it her own territory. I asked my mother could Yolvas have been a stronger dog by character if he was allowed to spend his childhood with his own mother, 'Very likely' was my mother's empathetic answer.

Just like animal species, human babies thrive under their parents' care. It is more than biological functions that serves survival purposes, it is in fact also about character-building and future-proofing for a long and happy life ahead for us. John Bowlby started his study about attachment by suggesting maternal deprivation as the major cause for emotional disorders.

In his study of delinquent youth, Bowlby concluded that those maternally deprived children were more likely suffering from social, intellectual and general developmental impairments. In their *Maternal Care and Mental Health*, 1951, the World Health Organisation used Bowlby's research to promote motherly love. Though it is important to focus on the massive effect of the parent-child relationship from the early days of human life, some psychologists are not convinced by Bowlby's conclusion.

They alleged that Bowlby was conveniently claiming correlation as the cause for the lawless consequence from the youngsters, since those children when being interviewed were criminals already. Bowlby might have relied on the boys' memories to trace back the first few years of their lives, but his retrospective study certainly spread out the fruitful seeds for future research in attachment theory.

Bowlby was not the first psychologist to point out the vital role of early attachment - Freud suggested long ago that the nature of the earliest relationships influence our subsequent close relationships all the way to adulthood. Yet Bowlby succeeded where Freud failed, as the psychoanalysis wasn't effective in availing the difference in children's social development.

Drawing conclusions from his research data, Bowlby found that many of the 44 delinquent children he studied during The Second World War had a long separation from their parents before the age of five. This allowed him to become the first psychologist to use concepts like *secure base* and particularly *internal working models* to make the attachment theory relevant to child development.

The attachment theory has given a great surge of empirical research, some psychologists claimed that the *internal working models* do exist. Other psychologists are able to justify through their research that securely attached children will develop into more socially competent adults, as seen in areas like peer popularity, friendship, empathy and anger management.

If we believe in all the claims from attachment theory, then 60% of the human population is functional and the rest should be struggling to survive with their partners, which is certainly a gross exaggeration. Besides, Bowlby's focus was too much on childhood, as a result he deemed the subsequent experience unworthy for our attention. For him securely attached children will feel eternally being loved, while the rest live in fear and persistent mistrust.

Many people use Adolf Hitler's miserable childhood to explain his future evil acts, but the evidence is that many dictators do have perfect childhoods, like Vladimir Putin. According to Putin, his mother fussed over him like a *mother hen*. Putin also claimed that apart from him, his mother had no other goal in life. Putin never felt disadvantaged or sad, as his first wife put it that Putin was his parents' *Sun, Moon and stars*.

One cannot be more loved than that and yet this happy child has grown into an intolerant leader. He bombed Chechnya flat and is invading Ukraine now, so the golden thread of attachment can be slender and fragile too. Psychologists might argue that power does strange things to people, so does money. But there is no shortage of kind and generous people who are all rich as well as powerful at the same time.

The tutor was happy and thought that I had grasped 70% of the attachment concepts, but the reality was that I wrote my assignment with lots of unanswered questions in my head. Regardless of how, anyone can write an essay without much conviction to a theory, especially when your degree depends on it. In addition, watching actors narrate other people's life stories gave me the impression that I was part of that make-believe plot, even if those stories might truly belong to someone else. My other problem is: how trustworthy are most people's memories?

A friend of mine with nine siblings told me whenever she talked about some joyful events of her childhood, her brother and sisters always claimed that they didn't remember any of that. Instead, they constantly talked about some unpleasant incidents from their past, while my friend could not recall those either. So memories are selective, shaped by our experiences later in life.

My friend is economically better off than her siblings, while her children are all happily married and successful in their own jobs. Consequently she might have nothing to complain about the predictable flux of her past as well as present. She and her siblings are undoubtedly living in two different realities; her ambition allowed the success that her untiring energy deserved, but the same can't be said about the existences of the others.

According to attachment theory my friend would be the only one exhibiting the securely attached child's characteristics whereas her other nine siblings are not. Could she be the one singled out by her mother to receive the sensitive and attentive maternal care while all the rest of her siblings were cast out? It just doesn't make sense and is not possible.

If anyone should receive some type of special treatment in that family it could well be the brother: the youngest and the only boy with nine big sisters. Strangely, he turned out to be the most vulnerable adult out of the ten of them. He constantly relied on his sisters' support after his divorce and became the least successful one career-wise among the ten of them. I believe their mother cared for all of them in the same manner, but sometimes being the only boy among many sisters can make a man less competitive - just look at the only male Kardashian among his billionaire sisters.

I remember once someone complained that these days TV was filled with impatient bossy women busily telling people what to do. There were Kim and Aggie showing people how to clean their house; there were also Trinny and Susannah telling us what not to wear; there was super-nanny Jo Frost to advise parents how to look after their kids and not to mention Victoria Stilwell explaining to families how to tame their dogs.

Probably womanhood is about sharing our knowledge with people in our vicinity to distribute awareness, but at the expense of annoying the male folks, and it must be the reason why my own brother was robbed from a possible successful career too.

I think my brother first felt that he had nothing in common with his three strong-willed sisters, then he must have been intimidated by the way we relentlessly pursued our careers. He was too shy to persist and hence could easily give up on the first rejection. Unhelpfully my younger sister seems born with a malevolent talent to never miss any of my brother's blunders, no matter how trivial it was.

She even made frequent announcements so that none of his failures escaped our attention too, disregarding the fact that our brother was too sweet-natured for his own good. My parents assuredly encouraged him with their gentle nurturing technique but the rest of us were complicit in acting as we did. We never expected him to improve with a sense of hopeless fatalism.

If we assign everything in life to genetics, aka our temperament by nature, then it will cause widespread unemployment among psychologists. In a proactive way psychologists are trying to help us to exert as much influence on the next generation through the role the environment plays. A theory like attachment may not be perfect, any more than other theories in psychology, but it generates debate and often leads us a step closer to the truth.

Even Freud's psychoanalysis, which sounded like a strange fit in the past, is now giving people a way to talk their troubles through with someone paid to listen. Hans Eysenck might argue that Freud wasn't the inventor of the talking therapy, but Freud undoubtedly developed it and made it very popular for the wider public to utilize.

The limitation of attachment theory is it tries to explain everything in our life with its excessive emphasis on early childhood, Bowlby even went as far as saying after the age of five, the child is beyond repair. As if our life experiences and choices we make beyond that point could never rekindle our inner light. Probably that was what inspired primary school teachers to deny any progress could be made by their pupils in subsequent higher education as well as their career.

Take my brother, for example. Whatever happened during his early days, too little attachment or too much attachment (my mother did spoil her only fortunate son in a staggering way, such as breastfeeding him for almost three years), he had a great family life of his own as a father. His relationship with my sister-in-law may have had many ups and downs like most marriages, but their love was enduring, crossing the boundary of life. So in the long life journey, finding the right partner is no less crucial than being securely attached.

When I met my nephew first time in 2008, he couldn't stop narrating of those loving anecdotes from his happy childhood and with particular reference to his doting father. I used to dismiss their family as a dysfunctional one as my brother turned into a heavy drinker, but I couldn't be more wrong. His three sons are hardworking and are all successful in their jobs with caring and supportive wives.

They must be securely attached for my nephew to enlighten me with his coherent autonomous narrative about his early life, and from what I heard I was able to conclude that my nephew is more attached to my brother rather than his wife. It is an achievement on its own, but I also credit my sister-in-law's devotion to my brother for his happily married life. They are unable to grow old together due to my brother's not so healthy lifestyle, but once upon a time, there was plenty of love in their living room.

To a certain extent attachment theory does have a lot in common with psychoanalysis, despite their dismissing each other as futile at an early stage. Since they both focused on finding out how our thoughts develop in the process of relating to others; they both insist that our early experience is the source for all the wrongs in our adult life.

For people suffering from relationship issues, attachment theory claims they are insecurely attached and consequently become dismissive and even avoidant towards emotional problems. I have no doubt that everyone knows about the all too familiar *defence mechanisms* which psychoanalysts always used to blame us for blocking our unpleasant memories from the past.

They both focus on the emotional connection between mother and babies, but attachment theory tends to talk about the mother's sensitivity or warmth towards her baby, meanwhile psychoanalysis encourages mothers to develop the *ability to contain her infant's feeling.* When I find this type of psychoanalytic jargon not fluent to comprehend, I usually go back to attachment theory for a clearer definition. It is the scientific one between the two theories, and purely relies on the data from observed human behaviour as well as discourse to define the outcome.

My obsession with psychotherapy started when I was forced into their orbit, otherwise I am not a person who would willingly talk about my problems to a stranger, psychotherapists included. I seem to have managed to shelve all my life problems so far, definitely not before asking my family members and even friends to lend me a sympathetic ear so I could get my whining and complaining out of my chest.

My lone fear in life is always about being misunderstood, and how can you manage to deliver all your troubles in a couple of hours to someone having a completely different upbringing and experience, not to mention perspective from you? Worst of all was that the psychotherapist was already given a list of my misconduct before she even knew what I look like, which should be neither here nor there. In short, the NHS does not have the financial resources to deal with a fully functional person, so you can only be a tangled-up individual in desperate need for referral.

It was German writer Johan Wolfgang van Goethe who said that *misunderstandings and lethargy perhaps produce more wrong in the world than deceit and malice do.* Probably that was why the young Werther had to leave the world tragically in a hurry to make his sorrow clear to the entire universe, but most of us simply must continue our lives with some form of misinformation about us floating around.

I remember once the Home Office refused to extend my niece's visa on the grounds that she hadn't paid her university tuition fee in full. The truth was that she was given a 10% discount for paying her master's degree tuition fee before a given date. I went to represent her successfully in a tribunal and the judge ordered the Home Office to grant my niece the visa to complete her degree course.

Prior to the trial, I contacted a solicitor to take up the case, but he refused to come and discuss the case over a lavish dinner I had prepared for him, instead insisting to see us just 30 minutes before we face the judge. Not willing to risk him further confounding the misunderstanding, I braved the court and was finally able to expose the error from the Home Office, which cleared the air for my niece to get her master's degree before she took up a post in a Canadian bank later.

Even those who spent days, months and years with a psychotherapist could still remain misunderstood and receive the wrong advice, let alone my less than two hours' encounter with a cantankerous as well as obstructive therapist. Looking back now I can see that part of the confusion between us did start before we met, as I was considered guilty by association with developmentally delayed child. Unfortunately it continued as the psychotherapist was unwilling to listen.

Instead of encouraging me to talk, the impatient therapist kept interrupting me with the intention to guide me to her desired answer. It was strange to witness someone with such tenacious determination to make me follow suit. Maybe the psychotherapist's personal concern about how to apply her not so universal theory interfered badly with the way she listened. Once the focus of her attention was lost, then the interpretation went wonky.

An important dimension of psychoanalysis is listening. Constant interruptions from the therapist do dull our urge to articulate the thoughts, which truly depends on a natural flow. I hope there are no shortages of psychotherapists to focus their attention to understand the human mind, for the purpose of making people feel the constant encouragement to deal with their problems.

The psychotherapist did present herself as God's little helper to me initially, in her desperation to validate her theory by luring me to talk in the way she preferred. But it didn't take me long to work out that she had an easily exhaustible list of categories to group people in, and I could be the one she struggled the most to find a pigeonhole for.

Still that was never her problem, there was always this secret weapon she could use to claim that I was in denial and excessively glorifying my past. It was hard to react well to such a shallow attempt, which she presented to me as a well-intentioned one, of course. The consequent lack of trust and her persistent effort not to reconsider her misconception about me, the so-called patient, could only lead to a very imprecise and utterly illogical conclusion.

While I was trying to make the psychotherapist accept my infantile history, as I was still young enough to get deflated by any distortion of truth, she suddenly declared to a startled me: "Your life starts from today". What a grandiose and even a rhetorical idea from a woman whose career completely depends on our past experience!

Besides, to ask a forty-year-old me to erase my past is as impossible as asking my 70-year-old mother to deliver a brand new mature me all over again. At that moment I hadn't watched *Eternal Sunshine of the Spotless Mind*, but now I wonder if the psychotherapist had indulged her whole life in Hollywood fantasies - the place turned Freud into the greatest psychologist of our time and made psychoanalysis sounds like an undisputed scientific study.

Psychotherapists like to think they are doctors though most of them are not equipped with any medical degrees. This hasn't stopped them from calling their clients patients. Or they might elevate themselves to the height of doctors for the human mind, but are they? For me the engineers for the human mind are teachers, since only education can carve our attitude towards life and pave a smooth path for our professional and future family life.

When I say teachers, I don't just include those working in the primary and secondary schools, but parents too, and we are by far the most influential advisers to prepare our children to face a challenging future. Our parental influence is eternal and unstoppable when it comes to helping our children to shine.

Inspired by Jerome Bruner's discussion about intelligence distribution, I see each family as a little community of its own in which we share extended intelligence. Probably in the opposite was the psychotherapists seeing us as the culprit if our children's development slightly deviated from the so-called normal pathway. When has blaming ever effectively sorted out any problem in the world!

We, parents with disabled children, are not victims. Far from it, since there is certainly endless pleasure and reward to be with these innocent children, albeit a different one. It is the world around us which tends to depict us as either casualties, or culprits who have created the impairment singlehandedly. There is, however, that adorable ability of babies to attract the attention of their parents by smiling, vocalising as well as clinging to them which is often missing from these children more or less from birth. That certainly doesn't stop parents to provide the necessary protection, security, love and food to their helpless infants.

Contrary to psychologists' claim that parents are only programmed to respond to their infants' signals, those of us with less communicative children are also hard-wired to be affectionately attached to them. It is not always a one-way traffic - you do receive their gratitude in their unique manner and often get thrilled satisfaction from their rare but blissful response. They too are equipped with an abundant sense of appreciation, though are slow in revealing it.

One doesn't need to go to a school to learn parenting skills, actually it is the first lesson we are given by our mothers as soon as we enter the world. It leads us to recast the love we have received from them to our children later in adult life. We tend to reflect on the magic of love from our parents once we become parents ourselves, and finally get a grip of their self-sacrifices which our offspring is demanding from us now.

The central theme of a family life is woven into the fabric of love, which transforms into a heritage of love. The beloved we once were are now enjoying all the hard work because of the abundance of love within us we are trying to offer to those mini-mes. Nobody is claiming bringing up children is an easy ride, but the virtue of love makes parenthood such a pleasure and an intrinsic part of our divine existence. The psychotherapist I met strangely talked about parenthood as a tedious chore, not a noble delight, that is why I assumed that she hadn't even got any children of her own to experience the sweetness of love. One can only treat such *unsolicited advice* as *the junk mail of life.*

Anyhow some psychologists do agree with Bowlby when it comes to language development, since study after study indicates the impaired child development of the institutionalised orphans, who very often talk late too. But those researchers also concluded that it is mainly because of the lack of stimulation rather than the attachment which left these children underdeveloped.

These days orphaned children are always being adopted by loving foster parents in the West, so they are able to grow up with affectionate care and encouragement. But the many Romanian orphans adopted by families in the UK did exhibit some type of language impairment and others even suffering from autism. Once again, the fact of deprivation from maternal love was blamed for all their problems.

Conversely some psychologists believe that these children were very likely being abandoned by their biological parents mainly because of their developmental issues to start with, not completely the result for the poverty of that era. It is like those Chinese girls being adopted at that period by the families here were left orphaned simply because of their gender.

Out of all the definitions about psychology, I like the one that claims it is a scientific study of mind, behaviour and experience most. The emphasis here is on experience, this is the one thing that shapes our mind as much as our DNA.

Although psychoanalysis might consider itself as a practice rooted in exploring our experiences, they deficiently are only interested in one aspect of our experience, that is the first five years of our lives. The way they over process the information narrowly from that short period of human life gave them no chance to explore the human trajectory successfully.

Years before my Open University studies, a book written by an American scientist ignited my sense of searching and discovery in psychology. Looking back, I could see the author mostly used evolutionary psychology to make his point. He talked about Harlow's monkey preferring a soft dummy instead of a wired one, though omitted that they grew into incompetent mothers. He also claimed a society that gives teenagers sexual freedom are less violent and concluded his book by saying let's hug our offspring tightly for a better world in the future. His western view of our life journey definitely has many supporters.

In a discussion about attachment in the Open University, I talked about the obvious emphasis placed on maternal love throughout all the world, but a classmate of mine disagreed. With a blue-eyed stare at my dark hair and olive skin, she stopped short to trash Islamic culture further. Given it was only eight years after September 11, I could understand what she truly implied with her prejudiced outlook.

After all, I was in no mood to discuss any other topic apart from attachment theory with her. Enter the war on terror, she would arguably declare that all western leaders were brought up by their lovingly white mothers with proper attachment. Could this too justify the detention of the so-called terrorists without trial, and the use of torture against them?

Attachment alone could only amount to so much for child development. I studied the decisive points of the theory and concluded it did manifest or externalise many valuable insights about how to help our young to thrive. Unfortunately, there is a sore point in all theories and that allowed the psychotherapists to deplore what lies beneath or is even non-existent for her own sake than by virtue of its benefit for concerned parents. A theory which was developed to help us to find the right way to communicate with our infant children is suddenly surrounded by implacable mystification in particular.

By the time the Donald Winnicott Centre eventually replaced their psychotherapist's lead assessment team with a paediatrician-centred team, I was told by the special needs teacher in the first primary school Bella attended that they had already tormented many innocent parents with their heavy-handed approach. A menacing world for new parents is also a tragic world to babies.

I am glad I didn't have to contribute to the psychotherapist's departure with my own complaint; by ignoring the appointment I had a sense of achievement over her intended control already. Not that I never made any complaints in my life, as I didn't hesitate when I complained about Bella's mistreatment in her early education, as any mother would. I also completed my husband's death wish to raise the issue of the medical negligence he received during his cancer treatment, as my husband didn't wish the other cancer patients to be treated in the same manner.

I did receive an apology from the hospital and was promised improvement in communication with cancer patients in the future. To my delight, I was asked for permission to have my complaint letter circulated among the hospital doctors to raise awareness of this issue, which I happily obliged.

Incidentally in this case I didn't have to act as such, since the serious misconduct of the psychotherapist couldn't persist without being cancelled. What surprised me was that she remained in such high demand and was able to start another job in Tavistock Centre straight away, hopefully with more compassion and without her frequently irate glance.

As a *geriatric* new mother (a friend called me that as I was in my late thirties already), I might be able to give those not even loosely connected theories a cold rebuff, but it could mortify younger mothers and particularly prevent those young and single mothers into questioning the sanity of the so-called specialists. The unnecessary guilt placed upon them can definitely turn them from loving mothers to depressed and finally unresponsive parents. The centre, which is supposedly designated to foster child development, would actually contrive to shift the whole burden of guilt upon parents with child developmental issues.

Sadly, there wasn't a single positive comment from me to add to the new team I met later. They also failed in helping me to improve my awareness of the manifold conditions of parenthood. It is my parents' loving care that inspired me to follow their example to provide sensitive and responsive care for my daughters. All this I was able to theorise in my Open University years.

I did consult my parents in bewilderment when my children were young and markedly different. I expressed my amplified worries about Bella's babyish behaviour during a telephone conversation with my father. Listening to the fact that Bella's five-year-old classmates were ready to engage in adult conversations with me about the TV sitcom *Friends* which their mothers seemed not to mind them watching, Father told me that we mature late without further elaborating.

It was my light bulb moment, with flashbacks from my own childhood. I was a late developer by any standard, constantly living out the fantasy lives of the characters from those Central Asian and Chinese mythology I couldn't stop reading. Doing math and writing essays with clear definition may be my strength or simply my pleasure, but it was in emotional intelligence I was lagging far behind my peers as well as my siblings.

I must have been an earthly mother already when I was finally able to stop indulging in my magnificent otherworldly dreams. In addition, allowing Bella to carry on watching *Sesame Street* and *Pingu* all the way to her GCSE years with Esin must have left Bella only competent in her social interaction by the time she was a university student. Not least because her classmates were enjoying *Sex and The City* when they were barely eleven years old.

Who could expect the admixture of psychoanalysis and attachment to be so toxic! I think to present a useful theory responsibly is not something the psychotherapist I met could do best, since she was too busy defending her own profession. A profession she was probably not fully convinced in herself. Using the right word candidly was never her strong point; instead, she expressed her opinion forcefully, judgementally, and never ethically.

Her single-minded inclination may have blinded her from the menacing hurt I received from her, which my kind and all-forgiving husband considered was her way to discover the worst in me. So it was alright for the psychotherapist to agitate anyone for the purpose of seeing through her own eyes how one acts in situation of despair.

In her jaded mind all mothers must have an inborn tendency to impulsiveness, and all she needed was to provoke us to unleash it. What she didn't know was that we were so concerned of our children's development and certainly in no mood to participate in her games, falsely or not. What also surprised me was that she was never aware of the fact that we were free to ignore her as I finally did.

Attachment isn't a hotly contested theory, it is truly a very useful human behaviour psychologists discovered during their tireless research. It only became an issue when a psychotherapist decided to misuse it to satisfy her drama queen alter ego. No wonder Erich Auerbach declared in *Mimesis* that only a priest, a teacher and a psychologist could be emotionless to human suffering.

Though Auerbach did leniently justify their aloofness as the necessity to accomplish their rescue mission directly and practically. According to Auerbach, priests, teachers, and psychologists may have to adopt this steely attitude to get on with their job rather than to betray their true feelings. If it was true, then my husband could be right and the psychotherapist was trying to be professional.

Then the missing part would be the famous transfer which is supposed to happen during successful therapeutic sessions. From all I understood, what makes psychoanalysis plausible is that the psychotherapists should feel our pain and engage with us through their newly acquired tender compassion. Now I also know that they must not reveal their true feelings by appearing arrogantly aloof. What a complicated world!

I was impressed with Professor Peter Hobson's passionate defence of psychoanalysis in his thought-provoking book *Cradle of Thought*. He presented a caring side for his profession methodically and painstakingly. An eminent psychotherapist himself, he talked about psychoanalysis as a method to study the human mind instead of a cure, but his desire to help people did shine through the vignette he offered his readers throughout his writing.

He fittingly quoted Gerard Manley Hopkins' poem to describe that *O the mind, mind has mountains; cliffs of fall/Frightful, sheer, no-man-fathomed.* He stopped short to quote the rest of the poem; curiously I googled and found out the last two lines he omitted which dealt with our misery in the purest poetic manner. The great poet's only cure to depression is to remind us of that *all/Life death does end and each day dies with sleep.*

To dissolve agonies with death certainly is not the solution a psychotherapist prefers, since their job is to help people to stay alive and carry on fighting vigorously. Hobson agreed with the poet that we may avoid disquiet if we hold cheap the heights and depths of the human mind, but he also reminded us about the pitfalls of persistent depression since *Not does long our/Durance deal with that steep or deep.*

In Professor Hobson's opinion psychoanalysis can attain its certain fulfilment once combined with attachment theory. There is no question that the depth of Hobson's instincts is still loyally under Freud's spell. According to Freud if a person hasn't dealt with the unpleasant personal past then he would repeat those events in his future life.

This might be true for those who are less attached to their parents also failing to bond with their own children, but can be a truly monstrous accusation towards people who were previously abused. It feels so wrong to hear psychoanalysis predict that abuse victims will eventually become an abuser themselves. That must be the pitfalls of psychoanalysis and the reason for its widespread rejection based on this type of acidic observation.

Life could well be repetitive on many levels, but never in a self-defeating sense. The world has become a better place because people are willing to share the exposition of their historic suffering and bring out more clearly all signs of abuse to alarm the next generation.

What gives Professor Hobson the confidence to declare that the combination of attachment theory and psychoanalysis is crucial in explaining child development is his understanding that life arises from communication.

For Hobson thinking doesn't just happen inside our head on its own, it starts between the minds when we rub our brains against each other's. He particularly talked about that first spark which initiated the thought, it begins with mothers' (very often mothers, but can be fathers too) tireless encouragement and face to face cooing.

Obviously this is one interpretation of child development out of many, but all theories do overlap and complement each other at times, particularly when it comes to children's social development. So ultimately it does boil down to personal effort on how much time we put to polish our infants' mind. And it can only be a good thing to encourage new parents to be always on their infants' side.

As Hobson claimed, this close attachment will enable us finally to lift our infants *out of the cradle of thought and* enable our children to externalise their inner thoughts to others with speech. Now they are ready and one day will pass the torch by fondly enforcing as well as commending the attachment to their own offspring, then the cycle continues as is human life and our seemingly endless history.

The human spirit is one of ability,
perseverance and courage
that no disability can steal away.

--BuildMeBest

CHAPTER 5: DISABILITY

During a conversation with our GP I told her that once upon a time there was not a single disabled person in my life, now I was suddenly surrounded by many disabled family members. I made this comment in 2014, before my mother died after suffering a decade-long dementia. Two years ago my brother also perished after nine bed-ridden years from a stroke that paralysed half of his body.

Now Esin is the only disabled person I have in my life, and I hope she will be here long after I have gone. But whether she will live happily ever after does bother me. Without the concept of death, bearing with the image of being suddenly abandoned by a mother who had been caring for her every single need in the past few decades, hers may become an unhappily forever existence, no matter how long that forever could be.

During my teenage years I used to go to visit my sister's best friend with her. They were classmates in secondary school and the girl had a Japanese mother. My sister constantly talked about her friend's disabled brother, who was same age like me but hard to manage, like breaking all the plates in the kitchen. When I saw him the first time, it was his mealtime and he was fed by his mother.

What struck me was his half-naked upper body in a not very mild autumn weather. I started expecting him to grab the plate and smash it soon. Everyone realised how scared I was from the anxious way I stared at him so we were led to another room before I was assured that he was a gentle soul who never harmed anyone in his life. In retrospect, I can sense how caring the family was as he was taken very good care of every step in his life to make sure things didn't go frightfully wrong.

Yet it did. One afternoon my sister's friend rushed into our home frantically asking if we saw his brother. Apparently he ran away when they forgot to lock his bedroom door for barely a moment, wearing a vest only. Later we were told how women started screaming in the street when the tall teenager ran wild on the road with his lower body fully exposed.

He got onto a tram, which was the local public transport, causing women to shriek while rushing to get off the tram with their eyes covered. An army officer on the tram came to their rescue. He took the vest off and tied it around the boy's private parts to save the female folks from further terror, but the chaos continued until he took the boy off the tram to the police station. After a frenzied search from all the family members and friends, including my sister and me, the boy was brought home safely under the police guard.

In 1970s when Japan established a diplomatic relationship with Communist China, the Japanese mother of our friend could finally go back home to visit her relatives there. It was a strange time, when Japan was considered so well-developed while no family in China could even afford a TV set.

The mother took her disabled son on her first trip to Japan, with the hope that Japanese medical advances could offer him a cure. Of course, a cure for mental disorders is still elusive on any part of our planet today. Later the entire family emigrated to Japan and then settled in Tokyo, thus we completely lost all contact with them.

Finally my sister's friend came to visit me in London during 2017, immediately I inquired about his brother's well-being. I was told he had an eventful but lucky life, including a fortunate escape from a car crash without a scratch. But he finally died of natural causes about five years ago in his late fifties. I knew our friend's Japanese mother also died so I was eager to know who left first; as I had suspected her disabled brother died six months after his caring mother disappeared from his life.

I commended our friend about the wonderful life they had provided for her disabled brother, yet she admired how Esin was skilled in using a fork and spoon to feed herself during mealtime. For her, Esin appeared to be far more accomplished compared to her brother. It is the power of education of course, Esin is luckily living in a country and era that enables her to stay in college and continue studying until the age of 21 years old.

My sister's friend is called Zheng Qiouju. Zheng is a common Chinese surname, from their Han Chinese father. Her first name means autumn Chrysanthemum. She was probably born in the autumn and Chrysanthemum is a favourite Chinese flower as well as a rather popular girls' name of that time. But I am really sad for the fact that I never made a conscious effort to know her brother's name, and always referred to him as *Zheng Qiouju's disabled brother*.

I think disabled people were nameless at that era, and I wasn't armed with a vision to behave any better rather than following the shameful trend. One of my classmate's family life was completely dominated by her brother's cerebral palsy, as a consequence she always missed school trips and regularly didn't attend her classes as a carer within the family. Years after graduation, when I asked about her brother upon meeting her, my friend told me with a relief that her brother had died. She cried when she described the suffering he had gone through in his brief life of less than two decades. Then suddenly she thanked me for remembering him, since no one seemed bothered to mention her ailing brother ever since we left school.

In my late teens, I started working in a textile factory in Harbin with the hope to accumulate enough credit for my university entrance. It was there I heard that one of my colleagues had a disabled brother, who was apparently born with a functional brain but lost it due to some trauma from his early life. What type of trauma and how early it occurred might be considered unworthy for discussion by that silent colleague of mine.

This disabled man was confined in the loft when the rest of the family went their way to school and work all day. He reminded me of Mr Rochester's violently insane wife from *Jane Eyre* (and she was not referred to by her name when readers were first informed about her existence). Unlike Zheng Qiouju, who was always eager to brag about her handsome and kind brother, my colleague never once mentioned his vulnerable brother.

I heard the story of the disabled man's prisoned life in the workplace whispers from those concerned colleagues who felt ill at ease about the situation. My reserved colleague was not fazed by his brother's condition alright, but a caring environment might have done his brother some good and thus could restore some of his ability and independence in life, which didn't look like a priority in his family life.

At the age of 22 I finally became a university student with a bunch of classmates coming from all walks of life. The shared experience made us spend all our break time expressing our gratitude for where we managed to be then. It always ended with me carping about the insufferable conditions of the textile factory and the hardship I had to endure once upon a time.

Some of my male classmates would loftily dismiss my working twelve-hour shift as a piece of cake. According to them if I saw their peasant life started at 5 am daily from spring to autumn months, then I would define the word *suffering* in my vocabulary anew. Then one day I found one of my classmates was absent from our discussion for a while; he was always the quiet one, but how could he entirely disappear!

It took me some time to find out what everybody already knew: he dropped out of the university due to his mental health. Curious and sad for his loss, I suggested to visit him with my best friend. She didn't consider it as necessary, but reluctantly came along like a friend in need.

First we had to look up his address from the class register, then we went together. He greeted us with a not very enthusiastic handshake, extra weight and a paler complexion. The handshake was a brand new concept, an odd gesture never practiced by any of us at university before. The disagreements of the lonely human mind bemused me when my friend who was ahead of me only realised a handshake was expected after he withdrew his hand in displeasure.

Now it was her turn at being left without a hand to grasp, but by the time she gave up he then tried again. Without descending into my usual giggle, I watched the two of them unable to synchronise such a simple action for quite a while. After I took my time to digest the live demonstration of how not to shake hands, during my turn I managed to greet my classmates in his preferred manner with my first attempt.

What a relief when we were able to collapse on the sofa to converse over a cup of tea! That was when I expressed my desire to see him back in our classroom soon. 'Maybe next year', he looked glum. 'Join the class 78?' I exclaimed in dismay, to which he nodded and assumed a vacant expression, as if I was resorting to idle hyperbole. Maybe my friend was right for not wanting to come, my initial sympathy started giving way to a feeling of bitter disappointment.

We were called students of 77, that was the first year to see university exams restored after ten years of the Cultural Revolution. Young people who attended exams that year ranged from 18 to 28 years old - the ones who were unfortunately kept away from the university entrance, up to an entire decade for those oldest ones. Though we entered university in the spring of 1978, a new batch of students were admitted in autumn that year, so the title 77 was stuck.

I never felt like a mature student there, since I belonged to the lower half by age definition, but we were famous without doubt. To get a place in the university under such a fierce competition became an honour and I carried it like a badge with pride. I never forgot to claim my year 77 student status to anyone around me, and now he was willing to relegate. On our way home my friend assured me if I knew what he had gone through, I would consider it a small price to pay at most to delay his attainment of a university degree for six months.

"So what had he gone through then?", I asked. Apparently he fell for a girl from another class. Then I assumed he was scorned and rejected. Not quite - according to my friend our Romeo preferred to suffer silently. Supposedly he would rather die than declare his feelings to that one person who mattered so much to him at that moment. But what didn't make sense to me was how could the inner thoughts of such a private person became public knowledge so soon?

To complicate the matter further, it turned out

that his love interest was busily admiring one of the numerous eligible bachelors among our future engineers (they did become an item - I noticed later). He wasn't the first or the last person with an aching heart from the unrequited crush, so why not remain calm instead of choosing to live such a miserable and forlorn life like an abstemious captive! The heart can desire but it is impossible to be with someone unavailable. Isn't that one of the sententious laws of nature in life?

Out of the many Russian folk songs I can sing, one was about unattainable love. Notwithstanding it was a girl who couldn't pluck up her courage to inform the boy she fancied. One line of the lyrics spelled out the taboo for girls not to take the first step, but the song was not a tearjerker. At the end, a group of cheerful girls playfully declared in their chorus to 'keep the men of our hearts guessing'. With its beautiful melody, this is easily my all-time favourite song and sang by my type of women.

Anyway this one incident had changed my idyllic impression of our university days: behind the lecture theatre, the inner process of real life continues unfolding. On reflection I also wasn't fully convinced of the simplistic interpretation of my classmate's mental condition. A fragile brain, prone to pain and incapable of dealing with sorrow, can be the product of some historical heartache too. That probably could explain my classmate's permanent drop out more accurately. I never saw him again.

So far it was all about men with troubled brains and bodies I encountered in my life; that was until Esin, my younger daughter was born. Esin spent her first two years being declared normal by our GP though we did notice something didn't look right, but like many parents we expected her to grow out of it. A happy child, physically fit and might also be mentally alright was our optimistic opinion.

Besides, due to their tender years, all in quite different ways, some children do behave like autistic until they grow out of it, since development is an uneven and very individualistic process. I still look at Esin's early photos and wonder what had gone so spectacularly wrong over the years, then imagine what a wonderful life she could've had with her sunny character and positive attitude towards life. If only we had found ways to stave off, or at least partially hold off her disability.

Life with Esin is challenging without a doubt. It isn't the usual school followed by work trajectory, and she will never have her own family then repeat the same process with her own children one day. The normal cycle of life is broken here, with plenty to discover when bringing her up. The one important lesson I learnt in life is to make Esin the sphere of my existence, that means enact our daily activities according to Esin's will.

I go to bed when Esin is tired and get up in the morning when she is ready. We always eat what Esin likes and it took me a long time to discover her favourite food one by one. I have managed to turn all of them into healthy versions of meals, which she would accept and we can relish too. It seems the norm in this country to send adult Esin to care homes to join the other disabled people, but I have chosen to live in harmony with Esin by obeying her wishes lastingly.

Esin was always reluctant and bitter when it was time to go to school, but the extent of her aversion to being anywhere away from home only became evident to me gradually. Usually after her parents' meeting in school, Esin would insist to leave with me instantly. As a result we always tried to arrange the meetings suitably for the end of her school day.

One morning I had to go to meet her teacher in Ickburgh school; when we got off the school bus I was told now Esin had moved into a new classroom. The teacher who was busy with other pupils confidently told me that Esin could guide me there, but soon I found two of us standing in the other exit of her school gate. Once more, Esin brought her latent desire out.

Sadly Esin's calculated effort to bypass her new classroom failed that day. To her disappointment I took Esin back to her teacher on that one occasion, but did try to keep Esin at home as often as possible, merely because she sneezed once in the morning. I am fully aware of the fact that she will suffer after me, so why not strive with all my power to offer Esin as much comfort as possible as I am fit and around.

Years ago, social services offered to look after Esin for me so I could go away for a holiday. What they couldn't fathom was that my holidays are to entertain Esin. Never in my life can I consciously enjoy any type of extravaganza while Esin is missing me desperately in a boring place being fed beans on toast.

My best holidays were spent with Esin staring at the beautiful Aegean Sea. Esin didn't enjoy swimming as much as I do, but she is fascinated by the vast sea, and staring at the turbulent waves at night is her all-time favourite activity during our seaside holiday time. We simply followed her there every night before bedtime. When I say we, it wasn't only her father, sister and me, but the whole clan: friends and relatives I invited to our exotic Bodrum holiday home all came along with us night after night.

My most memorable holiday was in 2004, when I sensed my 91-year-old father had very little time left in this world. I sat motionlessly staring at the waves night after night with Esin, occasionally noticing drops of salty seawater glided down my face, as if nature was comforting me with kisses and caresses, as the rising and falling waves gave me a ride to go back in time as Father's little girl again.

I could hear Father talked and sang to me afresh before he vanished with his soothing voice. Not everything I did served to amuse Father, like the time he took me out on his bike when I asked him what the handbrake was for. After I realised that the bike would stop immediately if I pulled the brake, I spontaneously did exactly that with all my might. The bike stopped alright, followed by somersaulting as my unsuspecting father pedalled on. We were thrown on the ground with my extraneous research about the power of the brake. Instead of blaming me for my idiocy, Father rushed up to hug me, to comfort me and was desperate to make sure that I wasn't hurt.

Father died in December that year, I found comfort by looking for him in the sea hereafter. The rather flamboyantly starry sky above the sea was also poised to ease my anguish. Gazing my way into the night sky, I accepted that life only shines temporarily before streaming down like a meteor to the other eternal world. The tremendous weight of the grievances slowly lifted, looking at how Esin fixed her gaze at the sea, I know the unseen journey beyond me will be embarked with a loyal company together. It brightened my heart to know that Esin can sense the magical power of nature!

When Esin completed her education at the age of 21 from her college, I was told that I needed a break from Esin by sending her a few times a week to a daily activity centre. Esin is a good companion who I am attached to the extent of considering her as my internal organ. She has especially become indispensable since my husband died. Her smile always makes me realise what a difference I can make for her. I never feel lonely when Esin is around.

Esin will be watching her favourite videos or listening to music on YouTube when I read or write. We do cast glances from one of us upon the other frequently. She feels safe with me, likewise I feel complete with her. Sometimes we watch our favourite Sesame Street episodes together; they bring back pleasant memories. I believe Esin likes looking back at her own life too - the way she stares at our holiday photos convinces me that her brain is capable of tracing back in time just like the rest of us.

The domestic harmony I have shared with Esin is partly due to her contentment. Esin need not worry about the fact that I would ever consider her as an enigma that can't be solved. Unlike the teachers who encouraged me to send Esin to a care home with ignorance and disregard, I will be concerned of how Esin could reconcile herself to the inevitable difference. In addition, becoming a care home resident means Esin will lose all her identity.

Esin's identity crisis was highlighted together with all the forms I filled to claim benefit for her, as none of the descriptions fit her. Once the Department of Work and Pension reduced Esin's disability allowance on the grounds that my answer led them to believe Esin was able-bodied at night, and disabled during the day. It was only after a letter from our GP that they agreed to restore the original allowance. Whether they accepted there is no such strange condition existing among the human race must be another matter.

In some measure, Esin and me have a united mind. I play piano for Esin every day, knowing she will never criticise my mistakes like her sister constantly does. We enjoy watching TV programs together, if Esin fixes her gaze on the screen then I will render it as a sure one from the impression received. For care workers, looking after Esin doesn't verge beyond the realm of a career, but for me it is frankly a life I have chosen to live.

Before COVID-19, I did send Esin to a daily activity centre twice a week. Although I rejected the concept of having a never-needed break myself, I followed suit in case Esin needed a break from me for a couple of hours a week. Always with a sudden moment of exasperation Esin left reluctantly.

Looking at grumpy Esin in the morning, I easily became too happy not to send her away once the COVID lockdown started. One day, as we walked to the local park, a neighbour commented about how good Esin looked now. She particularly pointed to

Esin's abdomen; I was obliged to assume that she must be comparing Esin to the state when she was brought back home by the care workers. There was no tucking Esin's blouse in, and no one could bother to button Esin's jacket either, which she undid earlier on due to her frigidity. Suddenly Esin started looking smart when she was out with me.

A year before Esin left her college, I had a shock visit by a social services worker. The man didn't come alone, he was accompanied by a nurse and two gun trotting policemen. Without introducing himself, the social worker hurriedly asked if there was a young woman called Esin living in these premises.

Confused and anxiously I called Esin to come downstairs. As though she was waiting for this moment all day, Esin swiftly came down to join us, and the nurse immediately commented on Esin's happy smile. In part, it was good luck that Esin and me were just back from her favourite restaurant, otherwise her cheerful presence could not always be guaranteed. Along with, joining visitors gaily is not always a thing Esin considered ought to be done.

Esin was kept at home that day after a sleepless night, but that alone didn't qualify a visit by social services with the weapons-carrying policemen. After I helped Esin sit down next to me, I was told that the teacher found Esin started scratching herself uncharacteristically in the past few days, so the school reported her to social services for suspected child abuse.

'Child?', I retorted. Esin would be 21 next month, and didn't the blundering social worker just called her a young woman? Exhibiting a degree of restraint, I explained to them that Esin always scratched herself. The ointment I used daily to control her eczema was only helping Esin to scratch less rather than successfully eradicating the behaviour. I also mentioned our GP once thought Esin had been involved in a road traffic accident, when he saw the scratches spread out on Esin's arms during the summer.

The nurse, the only professionally behaving one among the four of them (the other three men kept their menacing appearance all the way to the end) examined Esin's arm and also found a large scratch mark on her belly, then declared the teacher got it all wrong. According to her, the evidence supported my claims and no further enquiry was required.

They left. I was fuming to discover the immunity the teacher enjoyed despite fabricating all these false accusations. The thought of Esin sitting in the corner of the classroom scratching herself, with no one batting an eyelid upon her made me want to weep. How could I send Esin back to that college anymore! With one more year of her education left, I asked the learning trust to find another college for Esin to attend.

The way the educational authority dealt with my request was forcing me to withdraw my complaint. Worried that the phone conversation could be used as evidence, the social worker arrived personally to threaten me with his power to remove Esin forcibly from home. What a disgrace to see him eager to add up an obvious error on the long catalogue of mistakes social services have committed already. When social services stop practicing their moral and compassionate duty, vulnerable people undoubtedly suffer.

I could have carried on fighting for Esin and her classmates' wellbeing by taking social services to court, if only Bella didn't get very ill during this crucial time. She suddenly fainted before going to Paris for a mathematics conference and I called an ambulance fearfully. We spent the next few days nervously waiting for the result of her blood test from an in-depth hospital investigation. No abnormalities were detected, but Bella remained mysteriously weak.

Only eighteen months later, after another collapse, did a simple blood test revealed the extent of Bella's deficit of vitamin D, but until then we lived in angst of some truly horrendous ailments. Disconsolately, I had to put up with the incompetent college, and accept that Esin was to be taught by a different teacher in the following year. When her education was finally over, I was relieved but couldn't stop feeling sorry for those disabled students who had to remain there.

It was also the time I had taken up my second attempt to learn driving, after my first one ended with a spectacular crash in my husband's brand new car years ago. This time my enthusiasm to drive was drained away by the blundering social services and Bella's illness. Maybe I am destined for a simpler existence, since I have to now settle for a life relying on public transport only, or proud to be a member of the global elite environmentally friendly club.

Reading Steinbeck's *Of Mice and Men* I could picture Lenny 'walked heavily, dragging his feet a little, the way a bear drags his paws'. I assume his parents must be struggling to provide for the family when Lenny was growing up, and left with no energy to monitor his free and uneasy posture. Early in the last century, disabled children were considered too imbecile to study, as a result Lenny probably was left out in the wilderness instead of being educated.

Learning to walk in a straight line may not sound like a roaring educational success, but is an improvement from Esin's springy bunny steps. Esin enjoys walking with a bouncing motion, and at the same time can rock her body from side to side. Only by discouraging Esin from her energetic bounce, can we stop her from accidentally bumping on people in the street and hurt children or the elderly in the process. Walking like that can also tire Esin very quickly; as it makes long distance hikes impossible.

Yet the care workers were in no mood to deal with Esin's problems, and always let her stroll on the road in her relatively wild manner, which makes it impossible for Esin to maintain an upright posture. Consequently, I have to teach Esin to walk with a smoother gait again and again. Losing her already acquired skills is a recurring theme in Esin's life. A lot of Esin's time is spent relearning what she once knew.

One rainy day, Esin came back soaked through, because her care worker needed to go back home before her children were back from school; thereupon waiting in a shelter until the rain got lighter was not an option for her. Esin definitely has less of a chance to be comfortable in many unfortunate circumstances like this one.

There are no shortage of people imagining a tailor-made world for people with all types of needs, but pragmatically it will work out better for Esin in the long run if we can focus on those avoidable accidents. Rather than persuading other people to follow suit, I have been doing my best to remedy the ills caused by Esin's constant regression. The world would be a better place if the disabled people are taught at the same time when they are being looked after. But what I have noticed is that even care workers tend to look at Esin as a hopeless learner.

Esin does learn if we modify our behaviour. Before Esin was five years old, I noticed that we were saying 'no' to her so often, she probably considered *no* as her name. One day I suggested to my husband to take *no* out of our vocabulary, and guide her to do something else instead. Like the time she tried to put a worm into her mouth when playing in the garden, we opted to gently take it away and gave her a piece of apple instead.

A few weeks after we dropped the word 'no', a marked improvement became evident in Esin's behaviour. The less we criticised, the happier and more complacent she had turned into. Esin probably was rebellious like other children most times, and trying to insist on what wasn't allowed. Finally an alternative activity kept her occupied and cheerful too.

I always hear people joke about that someone has to be told when to breathe - that more or less has become a reality to Esin for years now. She must be fifteen when she started rejecting food with subsequent weight loss. Suddenly I realised Esin has a pointed chin which I have never noticed before her mostly plump years. It is a bit like when last year's dry summer exposed many hidden treasures in dried lakes at the bottom of no longer existing riverbeds.

After two puzzling weeks, I finally realised Esin

had stopped swallowing her saliva. A natural process she has been able to complete from her birth was now lost. I started taking Esin to bathroom to help her empty her mouth, so that she could eat. Strangely, the school didn't even realise that she was hoarding mouthfuls of saliva, we were promptly referred to the psychologist for the sudden weight loss. As always they inquired, assessed but I would be the one to come out with an answer as well as the solution.

Fourteen years on, I still have to remind Esin to swallow her saliva for the purpose to breathe and eat. Despite it being a habit made to go against her comfort, Esin still is reluctant to let the saliva go down her throat after my order. As her keeping saliva in her mouth is still being done, Esin also needs to drink more water to cope with her dried-up mouth from keeping it open for long hours unnecessarily.

It was only after my brother's stroke I realised how much saliva we automatically swallow on a daily basis. My sister and sister-in-law learnt to get my brother's saliva sucked out with a syringe every day when he had to breathe through an inserted tube. It wasn't easy and they often found him wincing with pain when their hands shook ever so slightly for a second. Luckily my brother finally regained his own ability to breathe, the two sisters of mine used to wonder where all those litres of saliva had gone suddenly.

This swallowing process is so natural and crucial for our survival, babies could do it the moment they are born, or maybe even when they are inside the womb. How a mechanism which is taken for granted by us all could become a problem for Esin is beyond my comprehension. What seems threatening here is her own survival, a regressively dangerous hindrance.

On her part, Esin's brain has never shut down as some autistic brains supposedly do. I could see Esin is also learning every day in her own pace, but there is no shortage of valuable skills she has been previously taught which are often lost. That is the challenge from disability, luckily I still get thrilled when Esin manages to relearn. It would be much worse if her brain stops functioning, then disastrously her skills would never be regained.

What I noticed from Esin is that she still swallows her saliva during the happier times of the day as an unconscious process. She only keeps the saliva in her mouth when she becomes aware of the action. Regrettably she may never return to that little girl who once was overflowing with life, she has been far better in following my instructions before this constant psychological mishap. Consciously defying the norm often begets antagonism, otherwise Esin could have enjoyed much and suffered less.

When Esin isn't swallowing her saliva, she also becomes a completely inert and unresponsive person, a mere step away from being a robot. Esin will do better if she can keep her mouth saliva-free by restoring her biological norm. But I do notice some other disabled people very rarely close their mouth, probably because of their inability or unwillingness to swallow the saliva. Or is there a physical condition stopping them from swallowing, like pain?

My tutor, Steve, from the Open University once commented about how disabled people possess more skills these days compared to their neglected predecessors. Gone were the time when the hardship in life gave people no chance to make a dent in the disabled world. These days the favourable conditions gave us an opportunity to inspire all those whose passion for life couldn't be subdued. They are educated and are unleashing their talent to enrich our inclusive world for everyone's immense pleasure.

Surprisingly Esin is very good at doing jigsaw puzzles and can complete them in less time than I do. I am aware that she has inherited the good memory from both sides of the families, but so far I haven't been able to find a productive way to utilize this ability for her benefit.

Esin's final years of education were regularly spent to discuss her job prospects. Could Esin stay in employment without understanding the proposition of the work ethics? Regardless, I was told she would be supported by another person. There seemed to be no expectations for a sufficiently positive outcome from the workplace, any more than Esin should exert her body and mind for no apparent benefit to herself as well as others!

Supporting Esin is effectively babysitting her, even if one is trying to ask Esin to stack shelves (the only type of job I think Esin is capable of doing for less than one hour a day). If this indeed does happen, a strategy to gain Esin's short-spanned attention or try to get your message to travel along her nerves must be found.

Some wishful thinking proposal was about Esin working in a garden centre, without realising the damage will be caused by Esin on a daily basis might take longer to fix there. The absent-minded Esin rarely attentively watches what's in front of her, as she never has to face the consequence. Despite my vigilance, Esin still managed to break a beautiful vase on display at John Lewis, just by walking past the aisles in the department store. The kind staff in John Lewis refused to accept my payment as they insisted it wasn't Esin's fault.

I can picture the knocked off plants and pots scattered all over the aisles. The collateral damage from Esin's presence in the garden centre would never give her a chance to be there for another day. To claim Esin is prone to destruction is a matter of fact, and her carelessness is always evident. Social services could graciously support someone with the level of unfeigned enthusiasm for work, that is the sure road not to waste their sorely needed cash.

What is really stopping Esin's progress is her lack of speech. A functional brain can overcome the problem of the language production system, and enable communication through signing. Signing is a language on its own without doubt, and it doesn't take a clever person to learn those ingenious ways to express the very abstract meanings. The simple gestures, which is called writing in the air by Vygotsky, always amazes me with their admirable ideas, yet Esin failed to grasp it and so did I.

A friend of mine was employed by a school designated to deaf and speechless children during The Cultural Revolution years. The school might have failed to find someone who could sign already, but my friend had no trouble to start communicating and teaching her pupils in a few of weeks. When I curiously enquired about any misunderstandings among them, I was only told of an anecdote about mistaken identity of a new female colleague as a pupil's mother.

Apparently children informed her that someone's mother had entered the playground, as they had no idea about the new recruit. Such a logical error, a mainstream school can also encounter. Otherwise life seemed pretty normal there, steadily for my friend to unconsciously signing when we were conversing, perhaps it has become easier than uttering speech.

Realising that I was interested, my friend taught me how to sign for mother, one just has to put the right hand horizontally under his/her ear, then make a slicing motion. There must be a cultural background for this, since no mother could keep their locks long until forty years ago in China (globalization has aligned Chinese women with the world now). I still remember that elaborate ritual for the bride would be to go to hair salon for a hair cut, and often followed by a perm for the wedding day.

Nature has its own progression. Han Chinese girls usually turned their hair into buns after marriage before the communists took over China, most likely a way to declare the girl was taken to the wider male clan. Communist women prided themselves with their short haircut like Madame Mao. She was rumoured to be suffering from alopecia, then just conveniently turned us, all girls, into her minions during the first few years of the Cultural Revolution.

To reflect politics and culture in one simple gesture, sign language is nothing if not versatile. I can speak Uyghur, Chinese and English, but only managed to master ten Makaton signs after a week's training. It was hard, so hats off to those who can pick up the sign language speedily. I particularly enjoyed the signing in *Four Weddings and A Funeral.* Hugh Grant's on-screen brother inspired everybody around him to sign, including his future girlfriend starting her chat up line with him by signing *mice* instead of *nice* as a compliment.

Life is particularly unfair for disabled people. After inheriting all the wrong genes from their parents with no fault of their own, then they will be plagued by man-made calamities. For that which can be said that human cruelty always dwells not far from their lives. I have sadly discovered that disabled children are the main targets for bullies in school, not to mention that some suffering and neglect can carry on in the care home without their deserved compassion.

When Esin was four years old she came back with a bruised face from the nursery she was attending. When I enquired about the incident next day I was horrified to hear that Esin wasn't really punched as I had imagined but kicked in her face by a boy. The usual practice is parents get a letter about the injury - in Esin's case no one bothered to explain it to me until I asked. I couldn't detect a trace of guilt among the stuff either, beyond my belief.

So from the early beginning I already became wary of sending Esin away from our solid and secure home. During the COVID lockdown, I felt very lucky not to become one of those poor people, for nine months unable to visit their beloved, unapproachable care home residents. The excessive deaths in the care home also alarmed me of the dangers for being there during the pandemic: diseases spread easily among the vulnerable people.

One heart-breaking story I read from the newspaper was about a disabled young man who died in a care home and being buried without his loved ones' knowledge. Unbelievably the family only found out about his death three months later, as the care home hardly made any attempt to inform them. The sad event was yet before the pandemic era. On account of such tragedy, I could never consider to abdicate my position as Esin's full time carer.

Living with Esin is certainly more fun in our homely and peaceful adobe. We travelled a lot together too. Like the time we went on holiday in Lyon, Esin and me climbed up to the mountain top to view the cathedral there. As I was enjoying the beauty around me, I couldn't fail to notice how much Esin was smiling, despite huffing and puffing at the same time. Since then we started walking more to prepare Esin to explore the world with more climbing.

For Esin's upcoming 30th birthday I am planning something not just different, but less commonplace as well as unforgettable. Since we did everything plain and conventional, now why not try the rest? We can climb the Egyptian pyramids or visit the Mayan ruins in Mexico. I want to watch the Great Canyon in America and may join rhino tracking in Kenya.

It is a bucket list of mine, an ultimate seduction even Esin will not be able to resist. She likes flying, wouldn't mind looking out from the coach, and can enjoy some walking too. We must visit at least one site each year, and add up more trips on our way. By thrusting ourselves into a world full of sightseeing and quests, our wonder journey begins.

Esin's fourth decade and my eighth could very well turn into the most exciting time of our life.

PHOTOGRAPHS

People always ask me how I communicate
with my disabled daughter.

The answer is all in her smiles.

Born with autism and without speech,
Esin is blessed with a smiling soul.

She smiles to me at mealtime, and
when I brush her teeth.

She smiles when I put her to bed
and even in her dreams.

She smiles when we walk, also
smiles back when I talk.

She is 29 years old now.

With always something in her smile,

She is assuring me that she enjoys life a lot.

Language is humanity, though I narrowly
defined it as speech initially.

Esin taught me that as a universal language,
smile blossoms with superiority

Here is the summary of her smiling journey
from she was four months old only.

Smile Is Divine

Smile Is Treasure

On Your Joyous Face

Smile Means Pleasure

Smile Is Content

Smile Is Approval

When Your Eyes Sparkle

Smile Means Grateful

Smile Is Interaction

Smile Is Cooperation

With An Air Of Ease

Smile Means Satisfaction

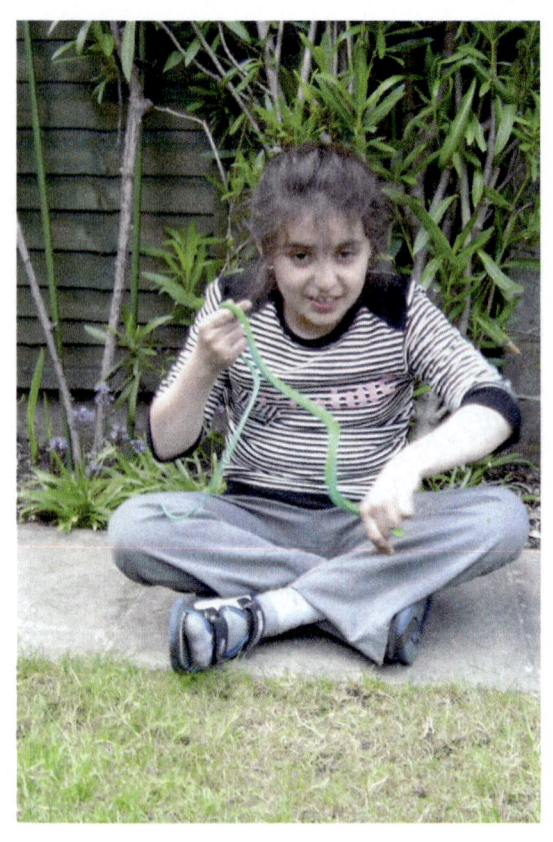

Smile Is Contagious

Smile Is Enticing

I Can't Stop Smiling Back

Your Smile Is Igniting

Smile Is The Way You Talk

All Your Smiles Mean A Lot

I Can Pinpoint Your Needs

With The Type Of Smile You Got

Living With Your Bright Smile

My Days Are Forever Sunny

I Will Take Best Care Of You

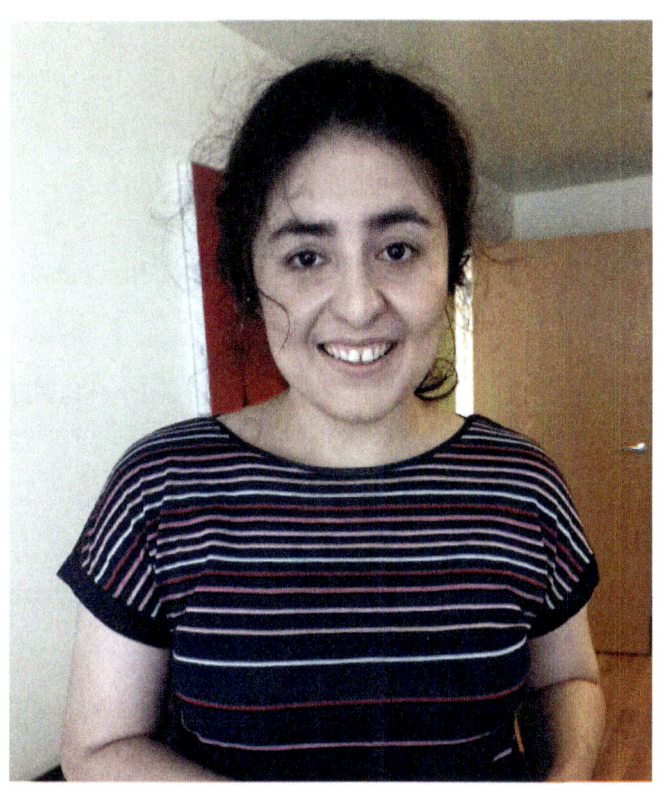

To Deserve Your Smile Daily

REFERENCES

Woolf, V. (1990). Mrs. Dalloway. 1st Harvest/HBJ ed. San Diego, Harcourt Brace Jovanovich.

Auerbach, E., & Said, E. W. (2014). Mimesis: The Representation of Reality in Western Literature-New and Expanded Edition. Princeton University Press.

Bowlby, John (1969) cited in Sharon Ding and Karen Littleton (2005)

Donaldson, M. (1987). Children's minds. London: Fontana Press.

Hobson, P. (2004). The cradle of thought: Exploring the origins of thinking. Pan Macmillan.

Eysenck, H. J. (2004) Decline and Fall of the Freudian Empire. Transaction Publishers.

Bruner, J. (1997). The culture of education. In The Culture of Education. Harvard University Press.

Vygotsky, L. S., & Cole, M. (1978). Mind in society: Development of higher psychological processes.

Harvard university press.

Mason, & Johnston-Wilder, S. (2006). Designing and using mathematical tasks. Tarquin.

Piaget, J. (2002). Language and Thought of the Child (1923, tr. Gabain, M. and Gabain, R. 1959).

Schaffer, H. R. (2004). Introducing child psychology. Blackwell Publishing.

Frith, U. (2003). Autism: Explaining the enigma. Blackwell publishing.

ACKNOWLEDGEMENTS

A book about parenthood makes me want to thank my parents, not just for being my role models, but also for giving me the best advice when I was facing dilemmas as a mother.

I also want to thank all my tutors in The Open University. There was Debbie, Elizabeth, Michelle, Michael, Mike and Steve. The many thrilling tutorials and fruitful discussions have sown the seed for my progress in child development and education.

My biggest thanks goes to my two daughters. First to Bella, the foremost reader as well as the editor of my book. Her constructive criticism is something I can't live without as a writer.

Last but not the least there is Esin, who inspired my unerring wisdom for the deeper appreciation of life. She is the cover girl of this book as a ten year old, also the motivation for me to explore child development. Taking her photo to complete her smile collection last week was my hour of insight to the journey we embarked together. The book is written for her, with her smiles lastingly imprinted all over.

The unusual motherhood couldn't be turned into a book without the wisdom of all the people mentioned above. I need to thank them all for being there for me at some crucial stage of my life, and doubtless had exerted their great influence in my thinking. When it comes to my two daughters, it is simply magnificent to be their mother

BOOKS BY THIS AUTHOR

Death Beyond The Jade Gate

ABOUT THE AUTHOR

Melike

The author Melike was born in Ghulja, Xinjiang. After travelling the whole length of China, she emigrated to the Far East with her parents at the age of two. She went to study in Harbin Engineering University then returned to teach in Xinjiang Technological College upon graduation. In 1984, she obtained a scholarship from the British Council to study in Imperial College. She lives in London with her disabled daughter.

Twitter: @MelikeEcin

Printed in Great Britain
by Amazon